CARLA M. HANZAL

CURATOR

WITH AN ESSAY BY **ROBERT HOBBS**

Modern and Postmodern Ways of Collecting Art

THE MINT MUSEUMS

CHARLOTTE, NORTH CAROLINA

2007

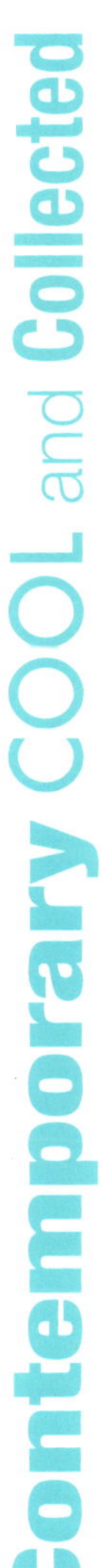

This catalogue is published on the occasion of the exhibition
Contemporary, Cool and Collected
organized by the Mint Museum of Art, Charlotte, North Carolina

This exhibition and publication have been sponsored by Goodrich Foundation.

GOODRICH

Additional funds for this publication have been provided by Thomas E. Kanes and Susan Valentine Kanes, Walter S. Brown, Jr., Emily and Zach Smith, and members of the Contemporary Coalition.

The Mint Museums are supported, in part, with an Operating Grant from the Arts & Science Council, Charlotte-Mecklenburg, Inc.; the North Carolina Arts Council, an agency funded by the State of North Carolina and the National Endowment for the Arts; the City of Charlotte; and their members.

Exhibition dates: October 20 through December 30, 2007

Chair, Board of Trustees	David Carroll
Executive Director	Phil Kline
Curator/Project Manager	Carla M. Hanzal
Copy Editor	Rosemary H. Martin
Curatorial Assistant	Kimberly Thomas
Chief Curator of Fine Arts	Charles L. Mo
Exhibition Designer	Kurt Warnke
Exhibition Registrar	Katherine Steiner Stocker
Publication Designer	Emily Walker

CONTENTS

ANONYMOUS LENDER

BANK OF AMERICA COLLECTION

DOUG BORWICK AND JULIE FRYE

LUCINDA W. BUNNEN

DR. J. KENNETH CHANCE AND ELLEN T. CHANCE

JEAN CRUTCHFIELD AND ROBERT HOBBS

DANA AND RICK DAVIS

ANN D. FRISCH

GOODRICH CORPORATION COLLECTION

ADRIÁN R. HALPERN

THOMAS E. KANES AND SUSAN VALENTINE KANES

GINGER KEMP

THE FRANK KONHAUS AND ELLEN CASSILLY COLLECTION

SONJA AND ISAAC LUSKI

ANNABEL MANNING AND MICHAEL KELLY

RENÉE AND PAUL MANSHEIM

LORI AND LIAM MCGEE

PAUL AND SARA MONROE

JANCY AND GILBERT PATRICK

PRIVATE COLLECTION, DR. W. KENT DAVIS

RANDY SHULL AND HEDY FISCHER

EMILY AND ZACH SMITH

ALLEN THOMAS, JR.

CHERYL WALKER AND JEFF HUBERMAN

An innovative undertaking, *Contemporary, Cool and Collected* offers a broad and insightful introduction to the art of our time. Drawing from collections within a 360-mile radius of Charlotte, this exhibition provides the public with rare access to exceptional works of contemporary art held within private collections. More than 20 individuals who live with and are passionate about contemporary art have generously made their treasures available to the Mint Museum of Art for this groundbreaking exhibition.

Notably, the exhibition marks the first time in The Mint Museums' history that a broad range of contemporary works from private collections have been showcased within the premier exhibition galleries at the Mint Museum of Art. (The Mint has presented works from collections of traditional works of art, including past *Carolina Collects* exhibitions.) This new direction highlights the museum's sustained focus on the art of our time. Such a focus is especially opportune as a planned Center

City museum will provide expanded exhibition galleries for a number of our primary collections, including contemporary art. This new facility is slated to open in 2010.

Contemporary, Cool and Collected boldly illustrates how contemporary art has evolved over the past 40 years. Many of the artists included in the exhibition are well-known; others are emerging, but are considered to be at the forefront of visual thinking. Curator of Contemporary Art Carla Hanzal has guided the evolution of this ambitious project, which encompasses 73 works of art by 62 artists. Her discerning curatorial eye has been evident in all stages of the exhibition, and her restless pursuit of great art—logging over 3,000 miles to assemble this show—is to be commended.

This exhibition is testimony that our region boasts a vibrant and growing collecting community. Many of the collectors have generously offered particular insights into collecting through their statements contained herein. Dr. Robert Hobbs, a lender to the exhibition along with his wife Jean Crutchfield, has contributed a thought-provoking essay on collecting the art of our time. We thank Dr. Hobbs once again for his gracious support, as he served as Curator of Education at the Mint Museum of Art from 1969 to 1972. We appreciate all of these contributions to this publication, which will serve as documentation of *Contemporary, Cool and Collected* long after the exhibition has closed.

Within the curator's acknowledgments, many others are thanked for their contributions to this highly collaborative project. I reinforce Ms. Hanzal's sincere recognition of all involved, particularly the lenders whose willingness to share their collections enables such a compelling presentation of contemporary art. I also applaud the generous support of Goodrich Foundation, the corporate sponsor of this exhibition.

Phil Kline
Executive Director
The Mint Museums

What motivates a collector to possess a work of art? Further, what motivates a collector to acquire a contemporary work of art that has yet to stand the test of time? Arguably, there are no absolute, definitive contemporary masterpieces, as such a designation comes only with time and canonization. Yet I have gained specific and telling insights from the collectors whom I've had the pleasure of meeting and persuading to lend treasures from their homes to the museum.

Without exception, the underlying motivation behind collecting has been to live with tangible objects that evoke a profound emotional and intellectual response. Collectors' descriptions of first encounters with the artwork to be obtained often sound a lot like falling in love. There is the intrigue and attraction, and even a sense of bewitchment as the object of desire conveys something magical, akin to an icon or reliquary. Sometimes the artwork is disagreeable, provocative or challenging—the type of thing you wouldn't want to introduce your mother to—but nevertheless enchanting. For collectors of recent contemporary art, there is also the opportunity to get to know artists, and to endorse and support their careers and ideas in meaningful and tangible ways.

Simply put, collected objects evoke passion and a desire to live with them on a daily basis, to contemplate them while eating oatmeal or after coming home from a long day at work. Such familiarity with the objects sometimes reveals new insights or perceptions, or even new ways of viewing the world. They are magical, and living with them enables access to the experience of the original epiphany.

Contemporary, Cool and Collected offers a rare insight into such works of art, which are usually off-limits to the general public. Generous collectors who believe in sharing treasured objects have made this exhibition possible. This undertaking is also the result of a creative and unorthodox approach to structuring an exhibition. All museum exhibitions are created within a framework which is usually circumscribed by a chronological or thematic approach. The peripheries of this show were determined instead by geographic proximity (all works must have been found within a 360-mile radius of Charlotte) as well as temporal limitations (all works must have been made within approximately the last 40 years). My task as curator would have been simplified if I had selected a theme and found works that amplified that theme. Instead, I used a treasure hunt approach, knowing that the resulting show, comprised of disparate works, would be cohesive through intuitive connections. In this way, the audience is invited to participate in experiencing the works of art and making their own connections and discoveries.

Although I did not utilize a thematic approach, various themes and chronologies can be detected. The earliest works included in the exhibition are masterful paintings by Hans Hofmann and Helen Frankenthaler. These paintings from the 1960s reflect a modern approach—essentially seeking a visual "truth" about what a painting is: pigment on canvas, containing no vestiges of a window-like pictorial space, the effect being immediate and optical, and sometimes approaching the sublime.

By contrast, works created after 1970, which make up the bulk of this exhibition, often challenge the notion of progress toward the sublime. Questions of how and why, and notions of "truth" and "beauty" are structured within a particular societal framework. These practitioners (generally categorized as postmodernists) endorse an approach that demands a discourse between the viewer and the work of art. By the 1970s modern tenets fell out of vogue, artists were beginning to challenge power structures, and the art world became more pluralistic, in part due to the civil rights and feminist movements. At this time, popular culture underwent a radical shift as TVs, by then found in nearly every American home, ushered in the electronic age, which shaped views of the world through incessant and highly mediated images.

The modern ban on representation was challenged in the 1970s when artists such as Susan Rothenberg and Elizabeth Murray began to use iconography, symbols and references to the figure. Issues of environmentalism and humankind's interaction with the natural world also became important to visual artists, as revealed in the work of Andy Goldsworthy, Josef Koudelka, and more recently, Wyatt Gallery and Edward Burtynsky.

The 1970s also marked a time when photography came to be seen as no longer documentary in its intent, but was recognized as a fine arts medium in its own right. Three decades later, photography is one of the most fertile areas of contemporary discourse, as photographers utilize elaborate staging or digital manipulations to create stunning, surrealistic effects (as seen in the photographs by Rimma Gerlovina and Valeriy Gerlovin, Gregory Crewdson, Robert and Shana ParkeHarrison, Anthony Goicolea, Loretta Lux, Vik Muniz and Sarah Pickering, among others).

Issues of identity, which became an important theme in the 1980s and 1990s, are addressed by artists Robert Gober, Kara Walker, Lorna Simpson, Alison Saar, Michal Rovner, Michael Prince and Lalla Essaydi. The relevance of place and history is also pertinent because of a pervasive sense of displacement within contemporary society. This salient theme is explored by Sally Mann, Phil Moody, Hung Liu, Andrew Moore, Jeff Brouws, Richard Avedon and Judy Pfaff.

Time-based art is also represented in this exhibition, including a sculptural work by Nam June Paik, who is considered the father of video art. In the 1970s Paik began experimenting with video from the perspective of a musician and performance artist. More recent videos by Liliana Porter and Janet Biggs, as well as a sculptural work by Tony Oursler, reveal different themes and approaches to this medium.

Collectively, *Contemporary, Cool and Collected* reveals salient trends and movements that have evolved over the last 40 years. It includes well-known artists as well as those who are emerging, but still considered to be at the forefront of visual thinking. Admittedly, the narratives of art history are constantly in flux. Definitive judgments on the greatness of contemporary work are elusive—some ideas and approaches, while relevant now, may eventually decline in significance and pertinence.

Contemporary art is, however, the art of our time. At its best it holds a mirror to society, revealing diverse perspectives and relevant issues. Like every other art form—whether music, fashion design or dance—contemporary art evidences awareness and an understanding of history, while seeking to discover the significance of the present. Artwork that can sustain a degree of complexity, so that repeated encounters reward a variety of individuals, is perhaps the hallmark of a "cool" work that has lasting power. And most importantly, the work must embody an emotional resonance that appeals to the intellect as well as the heart.

Carla M. Hanzal
Curator of Contemporary Art
The Mint Museums

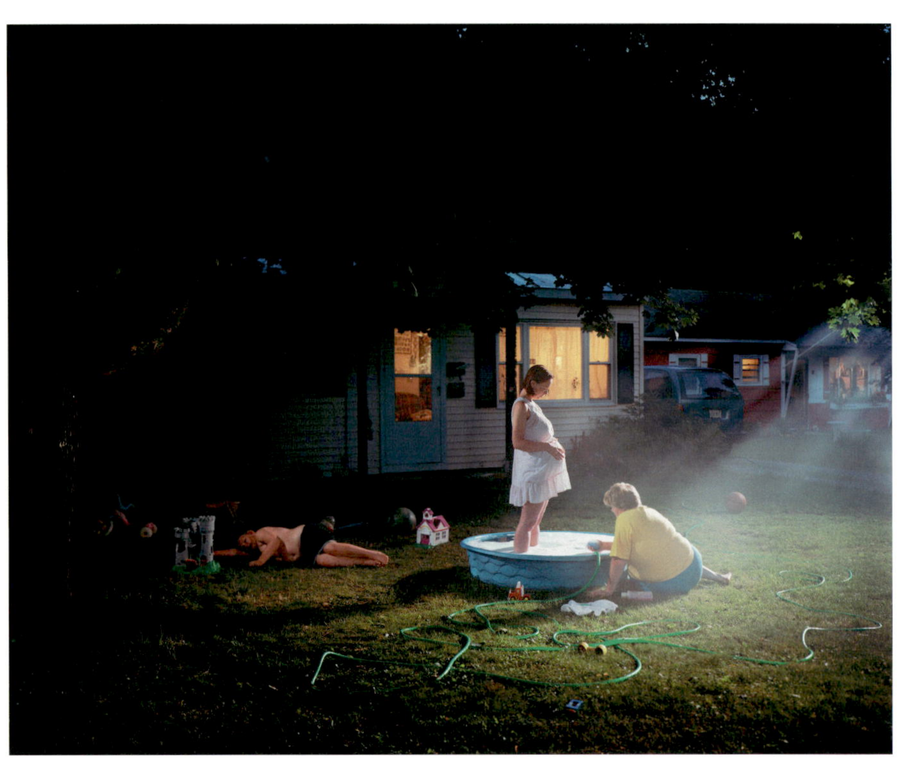

GREGORY CREWDSON American, born 1962
Untitled (pregnant woman/pool), 1999
laser direct chromogenic print (Ed: 10 PP)
50 x 60 inches
Private Collection, Dr. W. Kent Davis, Raleigh, North Carolina
Courtesy of the Artist and Luhring Augustine, New York

After surveying the vast amount of published advice on art collecting, I have concluded that an unwavering belief in the autonomous work of art is the cornerstone of most established thinking on this subject. The so-called inviolable (or stand alone) work of art has been upheld as a sacred value, and it remains the basis for most discussions regarding the search and acquisition of important artworks. Since this attitude has been so naturalized that it does not even have a name, I will call attention to its historical connections and limitations by labeling it the *modern* approach. This approach subscribes to a set of attitudes that are consistent with the values of modern art, which dominated most advanced artistic thinking in the West from the late 19th century until the end of the 1960s. It is related not only to modern art but also to the theories of New Criticism that were initiated in the 1920s with the primary aim of looking at poetry and literature almost exclusively in terms of their form. New Criticism dominated interpretations of art and literature in the West for a half-century from the twenties until the end of the sixties, when it was challenged by incipient postmodernism.

In the 1920s and 1930s the leading New Critics were all noted poets and critics, and they included such luminaries as T.S. Eliot, William Empson, John Crowe Ransom, Cleanth Brooks and Robert Penn Warren. These men were united in their belief that all possible meanings inhere to individual works of art: they wrote eloquently of the fecund wellsprings of specific poems that seemed to anticipate all the relevant questions that could and should be directed to them. The doctrine of New Criticism became so pervasive that Dylan Thomas would refuse to interpret his poems at poetry readings, preferring to read them over again in their entirety to make the point that works of art and not their authors hold the key to their potential meanings.

Certainly aware of the sea change enacted by New Criticism in which questions pertaining to the artist's biography and the social/historical/economic/philosophical nexuses in which artists and their audiences lived were considered irrelevant, the formidable New York art critic Clement Greenberg—the first to write intelligently on Jackson Pollock's drip paintings—became convinced that the New Critical approach to poetry could be directly applied to art. Rather than going beyond the specific work of art to meanings associated with aspects of the artist's life and the world he or she inhabited, New Critics, including Greenberg, wished to focus only on given works of art, their essential form, and the meanings that stemmed from an analysis of their specific rhetoric. For Greenberg, insight was equated with eyesight, and his theory of modernist as opposed to modern art, which emphasized the instantaneity of seeing and the immediate understanding of a work of art, was regarded as a dominant mode of thinking about advanced painting from the 1940s to the early 1970s. His theory influenced artists, collectors, and even museum personnel. Many art collections throughout the United States were based on his prescriptive theories about art's prepossessing surfaces and the fleeting moment of the aesthetic experience, which was predicated on eyesight alone.

In the 1960s Metropolitan Museum of Art director Thomas Hoving turned the New Critical view and Greenberg's doctrinaire approach into his institution's widely proclaimed goal to acquire only quintessential masterpieces, which were thought to be the pinnacle of artistic creation because they were most definitely imbued with the essential spirit of a master's style. Consequently, Hoving acquired the Bury St. Edmunds Cross, Velázquez's *Juan de Pareja*, and the Euphronios Krater, and he described the process of making these acquisitions as if they were a series of detective stories in *The Chase, The Capture: Collecting at the Metropolitan* (1975). Following Hoving's example, the current Met director, Philippe de Montebello, after three decades at this institution's helm, has gone on record as being most proud of acquiring for the museum Duccio's intimate *Madonna and Child* for $45 million. According to the rationale of modern collecting, which in the hands of both Hoving and de Montebello becomes an updated and secularized quest for the Holy Grail, no price is too great if a work of art manifests the right distillate of both an individual artist's style and the entire period in which it was created.

In modern collecting, issues of quality are of paramount importance because one must acquire the most potent and stirring example possible. Such a work is a trophy guaranteed to instill enormous respect for it, but it is also much more. This approach to collecting assumes that individual works of art assume the role of surrogate beings. Consequently, aesthetic and economic values are consolidated under the aegis of ontological views of art. And it follows that a modern collector must not only be a connoisseur— a person of rarefied and demanding taste—but also an individual who holds the keys to a given culture's vital (ontological) force. Having the discernment and ability to live with equanimity with such concentrated, edifying power elevates its owner to a rank in our society that is comparable to those held in past cultures by distinguished members of the nobility and high ranking church officials. According to the dicta of modern collecting, art adds enormous luster to the person owning it.

"But what," we may well ask, "if the ontological approach with the concomitant belief in quality is questioned?" What if culture becomes so fragmented that established artistic canons are challenged? Such questions have characterized Western culture from the 1970s to the present when canon formation is regarded as suspect, and the criteria for judging an unassailable masterpiece are subject to question or no longer relevant. Connoisseurship during the past four decades has been regarded as old-fashioned because it upholds the values of a superannuated elite out of touch with the contemporary world. And quality is relative, depending on the perspective of whoever is doing the looking. Since the late sixties and early seventies, the civil rights movement and feminism have had a great impact on the concept of a unilateral society in general and a unanimously agreed-upon artistic canon in particular. In addition to these two groups, other minorities based on race, sexual persuasion and age have further demonstrated that culture is perspectival, depending on one's background and affiliations.

Several years ago University of South Carolina art historian Bradford R. Collins conducted an experiment that demonstrated the extent to which culture is a lively debate, not a set of *ex cathedra* principles handed down as dogma. He invited 12 eminent art historians to look at the same work of art, using the theoretical approaches for which they had become known. He asked them to write essays on Edouard Manet's well-known, yet puzzling painting, *A Bar at the Folies-Bergère*, for the Princeton University Press book (1996) that he edited. The results, as one might expect, were radically diverse, making Manet's painting appear to be 12 substantially different works of art.

Collins' experiment begins to approach the problem facing postmodern as opposed to modern collectors. At this point let me emphasize that I'm not talking about historical periods but rather attitudes toward collecting any aesthetic material, whether it be Chinese porcelains, Picasso prints, or Karim Rashid multiples. Postmodern collecting centers on acquiring works of art with the realization that their meanings, quality, and even their value will always be somewhat relative and open to the vicissitudes of future events, the vagaries of fortune, and changing intellectual currents. According to postmodernists, quality is an aspect of art that cannot be fixed even though a work of art's place in the history of its own time is relatively secure. So rather than collecting sensibilities congealed into autonomies as modernists do, postmodern collectors look for chunks of history: works that are particularly representative of distinct subgroups and geographic entities, including but not limited to the global arena, particular nations, cities and regions.

If one would like to raise the stakes by collecting postmodern art in a postmodern manner, realizing of course that one can collect modern art in a postmodern manner and postmodern art in a modern manner, then one needs to be clearly aware of the slipperiness of one's standards. Such norms as originality are no longer tenable, because there are appropriators—people who take another's style or mode of working, such as Andy Warhol, who used news agency images for his silk screens, and Tara Donovan (p. 45), who reworks the quintessential minimalist cube by making it a conjunction of thousands of toothpicks—and re-appropriators like Gregory Crewdson, whose photographs bear an eerie resemblance to sci-fi films like *E.T.* that in turn echo earlier sci-fi works as well as American regionalist painting.

In addition to undermining originality, postmodern art can validate the importance of bad art by demonstrating that it is sometimes good art and even the best art, as long as it develops its strategies in a cogent and affecting manner. Premier self-styled bad artists include photographer Vik

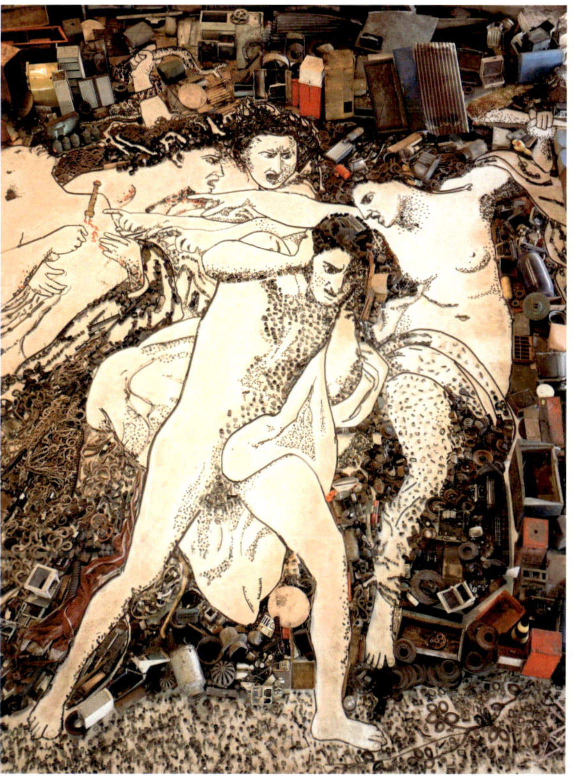

VIK MUNIZ Brazilian,
born 1961
***Pictures of Junk: Orestes
pursued by the Furies, after
William-Adolphe Bouguereau***
2006
digital c-print (a.p.. 2/4)
50 x 40 inches
Private Collection,
Dr. W. Kent Davis,
Raleigh, North Carolina
Courtesy of
Rena Bransten Gallery,
San Francisco, California

Muniz, who sets up elaborate assemblages of junk and then re-photographs

them to look like academic neoclassic paintings, and abstract painter

Elizabeth Murray, who combined elements of Chicago funk with the epic

sweep of New York School painting. In this type of art, reading the work

of art is almost as important as making it. When one looks at so-called

bad art, one needs to discern the complex and multistoried protocols that

include doublings and switchbacks that implicitly refer back to mainstream

conventions and different visual and linguistic communities in order to

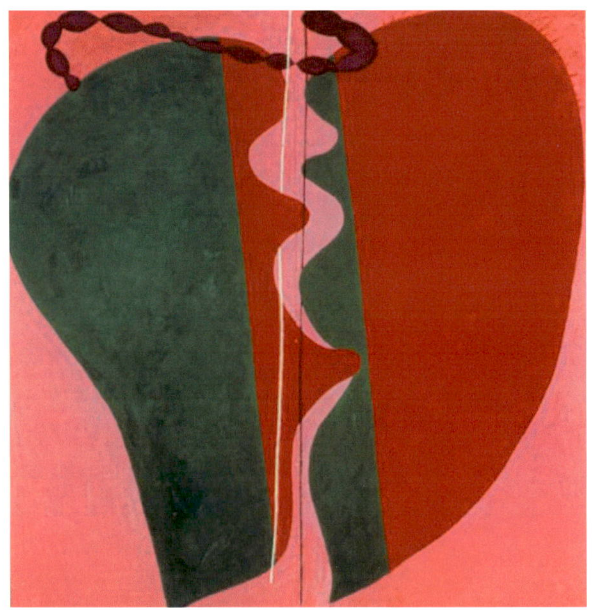

be understood. Postmodern art is not self-sufficient, self-evident and unmediated. It is carefully considered, strategically positioned, and often paired up with dominant orthodoxies that the work in question was created to undermine or redirect.

In order to collect postmodern art in a postmodern manner, one has to place oneself *in media res* so that one can understand from the inside how this work assumes meaning. This approach places a collector squarely among artists' power struggles over which artistic signs will define, even briefly, the present moment. Deflecting and transposing established sign systems is a basis of much contemporary work that ranges from

Janet Biggs' (p. 29) emphasis on the sub-culture of young girls to Lorna Simpson's (p. 133) testing the limits of the hegemonic male gaze. Such work also includes Richard Avedon's (p. 19) interrogation of the myth of the great American West by inscribing portraits of actual contemporary drifters in place of the expected heroes of Hollywood Westerns, and Robert Gober's (p. 61) revealing stack of newspapers that present the artist as a cross-dressing bride, thus undermining the cultural norms of traditional newspapers' society pages. Because of this emphasis on context and reading, particularly relevant postmodern works of art must be seen as documents and specialized pieces of information that frame aspects of the world in such a way that they choreograph one's approach to them. In this way one begins to look at given works of art oftentimes from other perspectives than one's own so that looking becomes a way of learning about other groups' sign systems and views of the world. In this way, looking at postmodern works of art in a concerted manner and over long periods of time, as collectors do, enables one to understand why the appreciation of cultural difference has become a cornerstone of modern society.

In conclusion, being a modern collector of modern art as opposed to a postmodern collector of postmodern art involves radically different sets of attitudes toward the charmed circle that collections often become. A modern collection of modern art is predicated on qualities and affinities between different works in a collection. The wise old adage, "collect the best possible works in the beginning because they will sit in judgment of additional pieces entering that collection," is a realization of the type of closed circle such collections entail. Predicated on distinct and compatible sensibilities, these works admit in their august company works that reinforce their special qualities rather than compete with them. Although such a collection may be eclectic, containing, for instance, both tribal artifacts and early 20th century French cubist and German expressionist works, it is based on shared sets of assumptions. In the example just cited, tribal works play an important role in the realization of a basically imperialist aesthetic that subsumes the aesthetics of the colonies under the aegis of the urban and mainstream art of the colonizers.

In contrast to modern collections, postmodern ones epitomize difference and revel in the vitality of conflicting views. Rather than looking for unity, their collectors enjoy contrasting works so that debates about rivaling approaches can ensue. In such collections the vitality of jostling and even contentious worldviews is opposed to harmony, which is viewed as smoothing over differences and therefore not remaining true to the actual course of events. Such collectors often pride themselves on acquiring discomforting works of art like Loretta Lux's (p. 83) cyborgian children and Chuck Close's (p. 37) self-portrait rendered in terms of sets of highly abstract notations that prod them to think about aspects of the world they are prone to overlook and to grapple emotionally with sensibilities that are at first alien and even threatening. For such collectors there is merit in being able to cope with tough works, and to learn not only about them but also from them.

Although the orientation demanded by postmodernist art (now entering its fourth decade) is well understood, its impact on collecting has been overlooked. No longer content with the unitary worldviews that the word "masterpiece" connotes, postmodern collectors invite challenges from many camps in their effort to understand intellectually and emotionally the varied worlds and sensibilities one is privileged to come in contact within the present-day world. No longer comforted by promising connections with genius, postmodern collectors must face the anxieties of knowing that today's meaningful debates can be tomorrow's discards, and the lessons learned now about differing perspectives may become the truisms of tomorrow. Not knowing a given work of art's fate, however, makes present contact all the more dynamic and meaningful because it depends on the time and work viewers must be committed to devote to contemporary art if they are to understand the distinct sensibilities works of art are capable of offering.

Robert Hobbs holds the Rhoda Thalhimer Endowed Chair in the Department of Art History at Virginia Commonwealth University in Richmond and is a regular visiting professor at Yale University. He is the author of many books and the curator of dozens of museum exhibitions, including shows at the Whitney Museum of American Art, the Brooklyn Museum of Art, and the Los Angeles County Museum of Art.

Contemporary (contemporary art) Art made after 1970 or works of art made by living

artists. It is a loose term that at times overlaps with Modern Art. Many museums specialize in showing art by

living artists in isolation while other institutions show contemporary art along with works dating back thousands

of years. Unlike Modern Art, contemporary art is not defined by a succession of periods, schools or styles.

Public Broadcasting System, *art21: Art in the Twenty-first Century, Season Four,* 2007.

http://www.pbs.org/art21/education/glossary_pop.html (accessed September 6, 2007)

COOL (idiom) The usage of cool as a general positive epithet or interjection has been part and parcel

of English slang since World War II, and has even been borrowed into other languages, such as French and

German. Originally this sense is a development from a Black English usage meaning "excellent, superlative,"

first recorded in written English in the early 1930s. Jazz musicians who used the term are responsible for its

popularization during the 1940s. As a slang word expressing generally positive sentiment, it has stayed current

(and cool) far longer than most such words. One of the main characteristics of slang is the continual renewal

of its vocabulary and storehouse of expressions: in order for slang to stay slangy, it has to have a feeling

of novelty.

The American Heritage® Dictionary of the English Language, 4th ed. Boston: Houghton Mifflin, 2000.

www.bartleby.com/61/. (accessed September 6, 2007)

Collected (adjective) 1. Brought together in one place; 2. Brought together in a group or crowd;

3. In full control of your faculties.

Phillip M. Parker, *Webster's Online Dictionary: The Rosetta Edition*, 2007.

http://www.websters-online-dictionary.org/definition/collected

(accessed September 6, 2007)

The catalogue is arranged alphabetically by artist. Dimensions are given in inches; height precedes width precedes depth.

Entries by

LAURA BICKFORD (LB)

EMILY BOONE (EB)

CARLA M. HANZAL (CMH)

SHAWN REYNOLDS (SR)

Patricia ANDERSON American, born 1939

Patricia Anderson's work is about movement: the movement of light and shadow and the movement of lines and curves. The energy of the sea and some of its creatures, including sea purses, dolphins and manatees, are referenced in this sleek, sensual sculpture. Composed of two entwined forms, Anderson states that *Combination II* "can be seen as metaphor for personal relationships, various stages of possessing and releasing."

This work, created from plaster coated in gesso and sanded smooth, is typical of her style, comprising sensuous forms and seductive lines. Inspired by her life experiences as a wife and mother, her forms caress and are literally bonded and inseparable. One form is caring for the other as it rests it on the leather pillow. Or it can be seen as two lovers locked in a passionate embrace. Either way, the elegant forms and satin-smooth surface entice the senses, conjuring memories of a loving embrace. S R

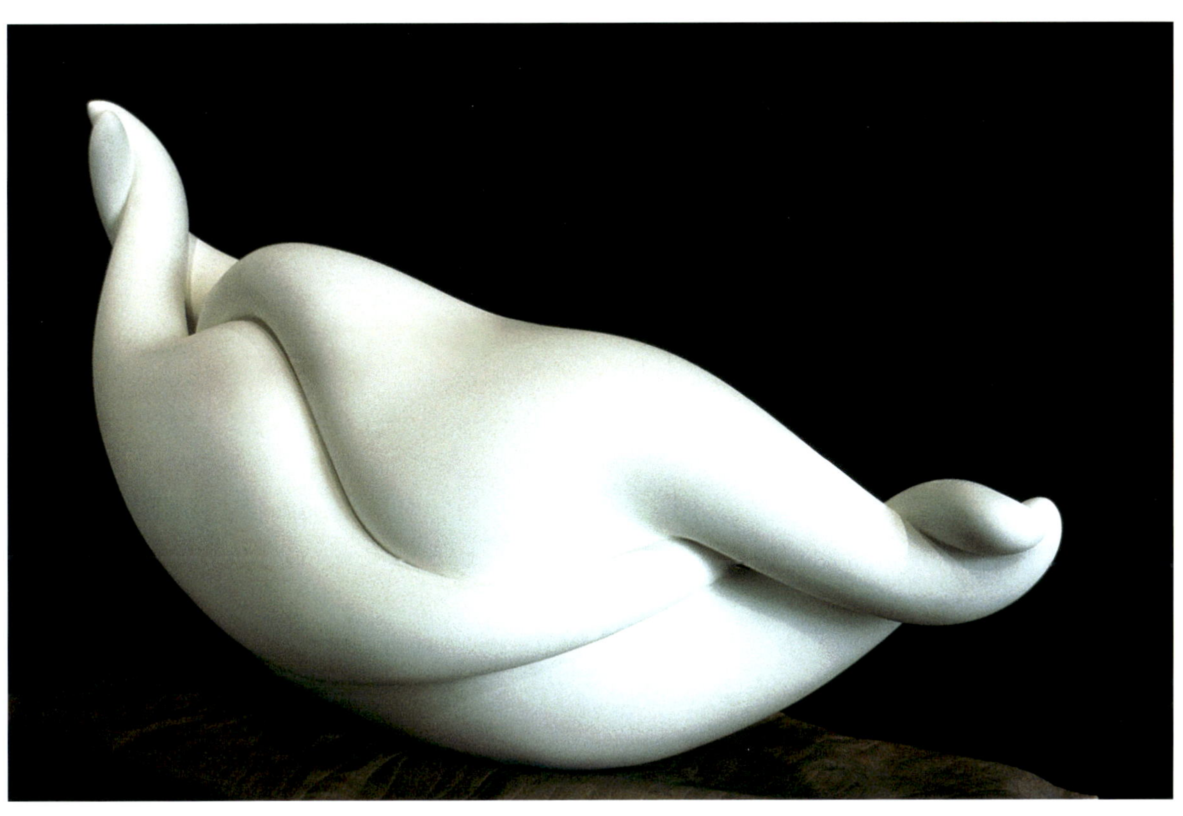

15

Combination II, 1992
plaster sculpture with leather cushion
13 x 35 x 18 ½ inches
Collection of Dr. J. Kenneth and Ellen T. Chance

Charles ARNOLDI American, born 1946

From the linear scratchiness of his 1970s work to the bright geometry he currently employs, the art of Charles Arnoldi is ever evolving. The somber tones and expressive freedom of that earlier work have given way to a more controlled formality that juxtaposes his experiments with color, line and shape, as seen in *Bahama*.

Arnoldi has described the radical shifts in his style over the years as evidence of his struggle to avoid the trap of repetition and his desire to keep his work fresh. For Arnoldi, staying fresh often means working in two different styles simultaneously. This piece is from a current series of fragmented arcs. Arnoldi has called his arcs the more emotional of the two styles, and thus the more human. His geometric wall reliefs reflect another of his concerns: the synthetic approach to painting that is all too common in art today. S R

Bahama, 2004
acrylic on canvas
57 x 42 ½ inches
Collection of Emily and Zach Smith

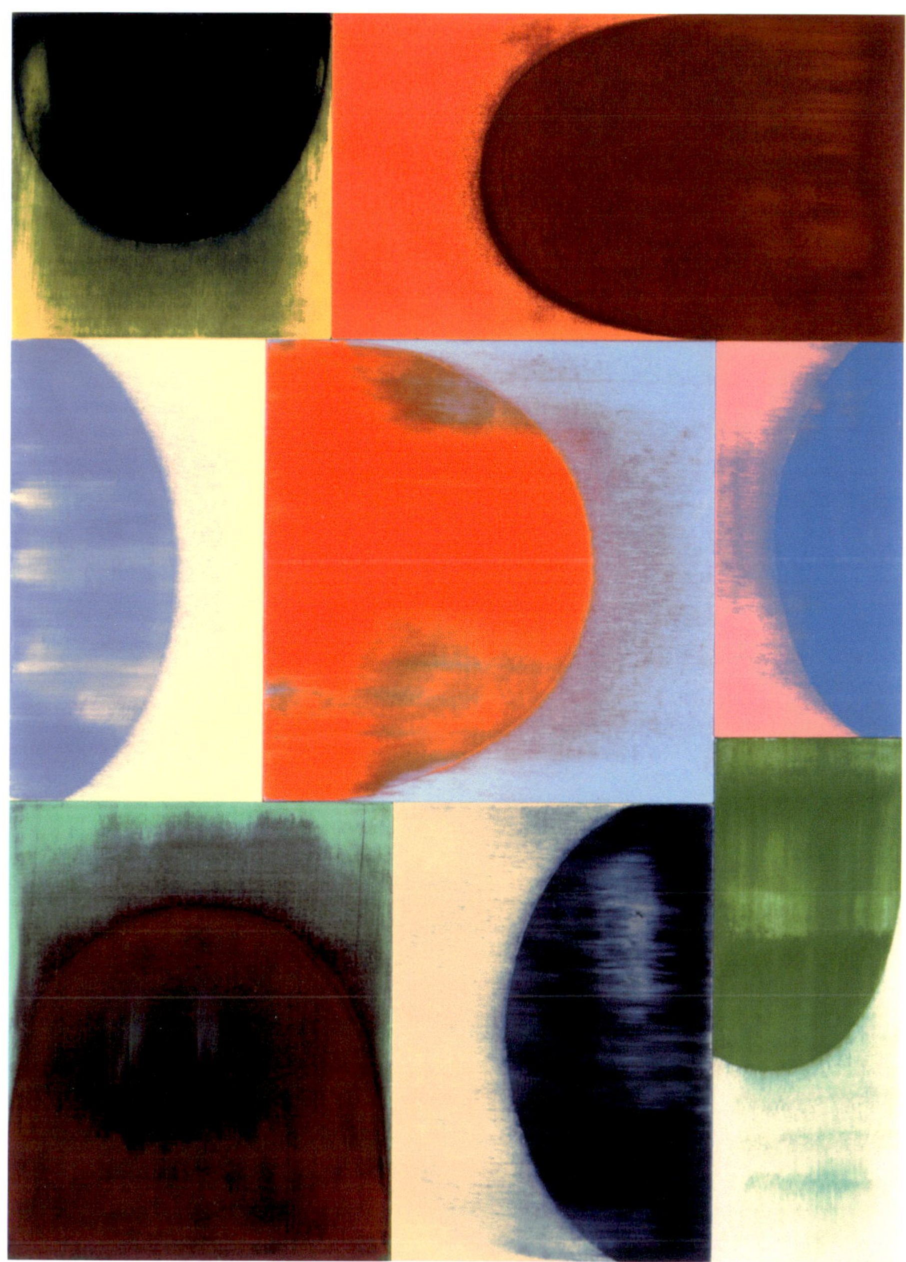

Richard AVEDON American, 1923-2004

Richard Avedon gained renown for his fashion photography for *Harper's Bazaar* magazine in the 1940s, but did perhaps his most inspired and personal work in the 1979 series *In the American West.* In the style that Avedon became known for, his subjects are captured in front of a stark white backdrop with an intense light that reveals the traces of their work and worries. Instead of depicting the cowboy heroes of Hollywood, Avedon focused on the drifters, waitresses, slaughterhouse workers, and farmers whom most of society ignores. Bill Curry, a drifter, is known only through the confrontation of this portrait, which provides the viewer with an intimate look at a stranger. L B

Bill Curry, Drifter, Interstate 40, Yukon, Oklahoma, June 16, 1980, 1980
vintage silverprint (edition 1/5)
47 x 37 ¾ inches
Anonymous lender

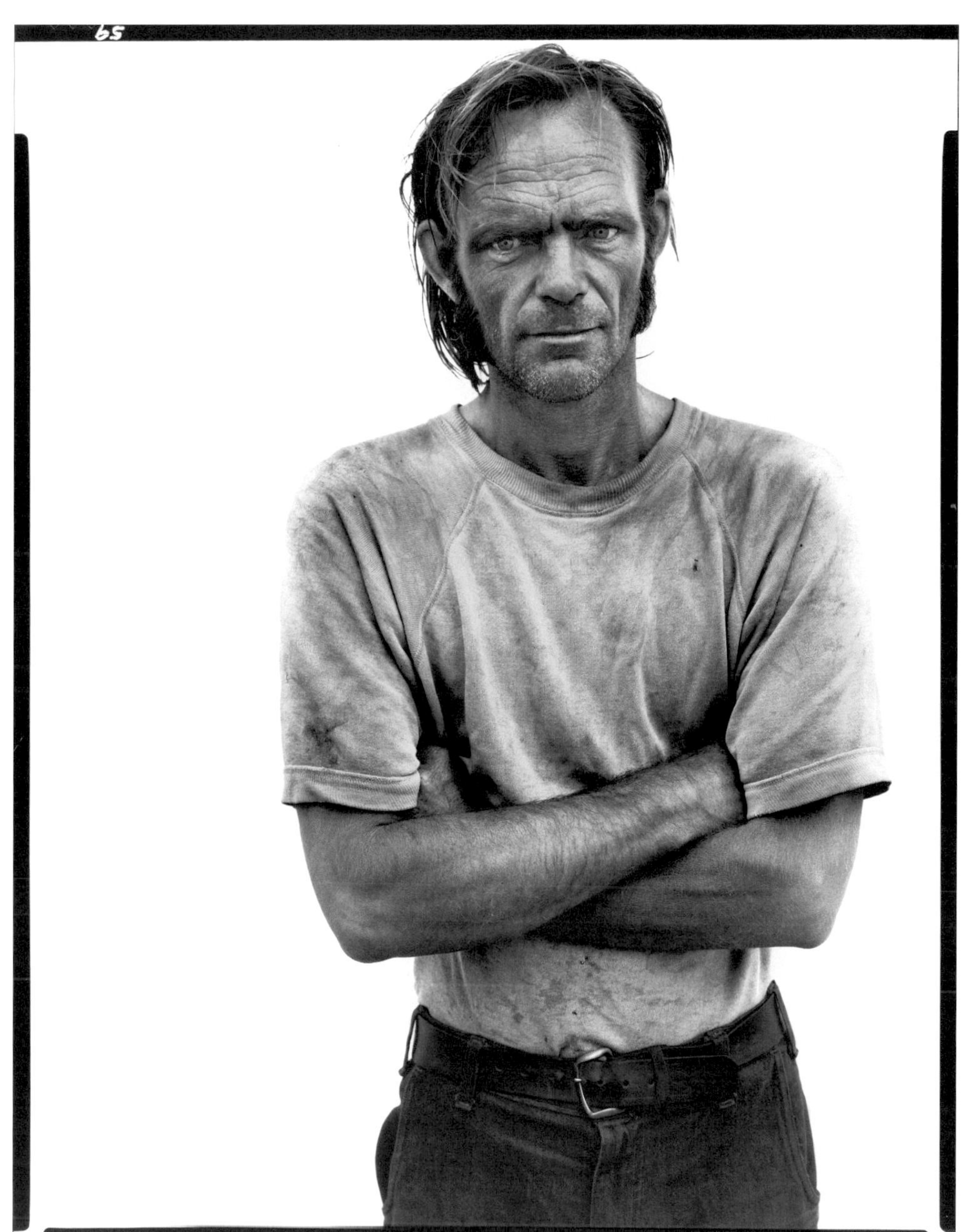

65

With an uncanny ability to draw upon and honor past sculptural traditions, but also to innovate and push the boundaries of his chosen genre, German sculptor Stephan Balkenhol creates figures that are starkly unemotional. Balkenhol often works in wawa wood, which he leaves mainly unpainted to suggest the pigmentation of human flesh. He works rapidly, which gives his sculptures a crude and sketch-like feel. While some of his figures are portrayed in isolation, gazing stoically at the viewer, others interact in groups. In *Trohn*, however, a man's and a woman's head share a body, which then transforms into the back and seat of a chair. The regal figures, which seem to be alchemically united, the chair, and the base for the chair are all roughly carved from a single massive log. The common material unites all three components into an expressive exploration of human connection. Strikingly similar to his sculptures, Balkenhol's drawings, such as *Untitled*, exhibit his mastery at eliciting the same response in other media as well. L B

20

Trohn, 2005
pigmented wawa wood
70 x 17 $^5/_8$ x 17 $^5/_8$ inches
Collection of Randy Shull and Hedy Fischer

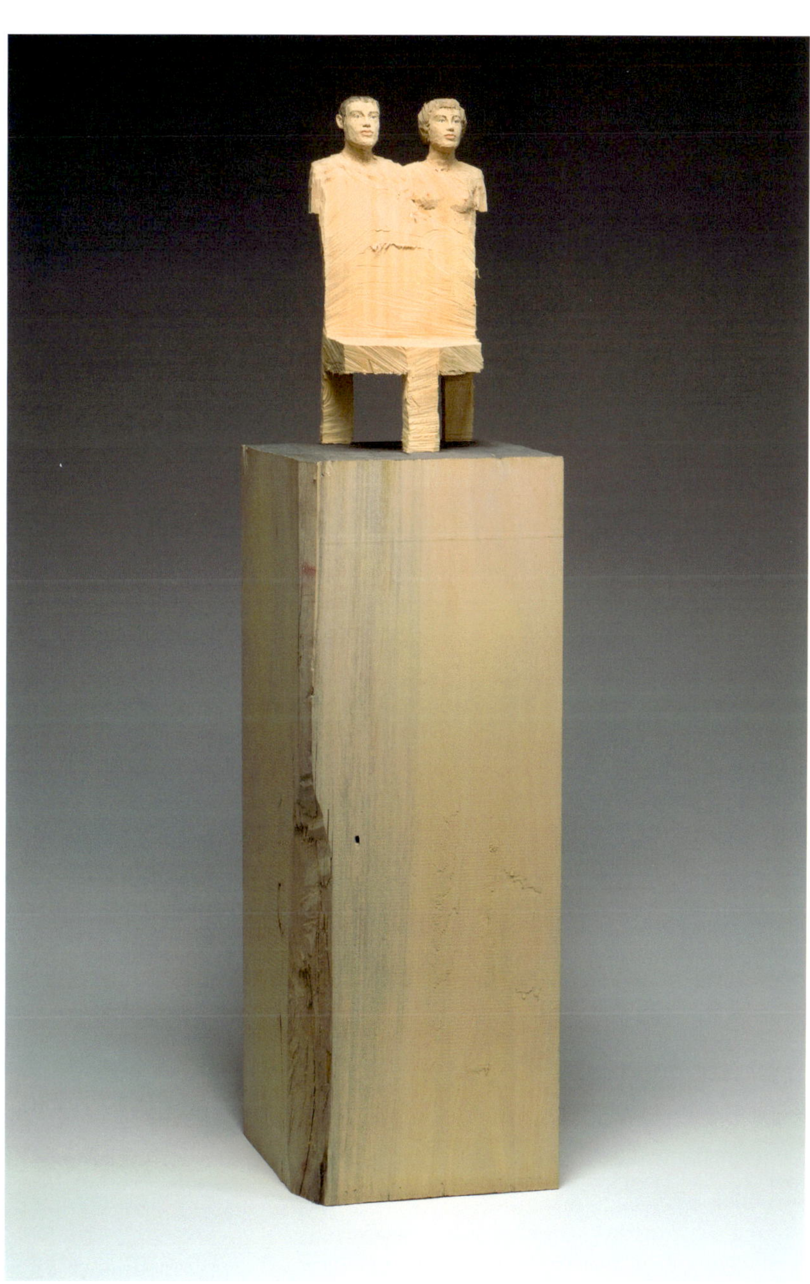

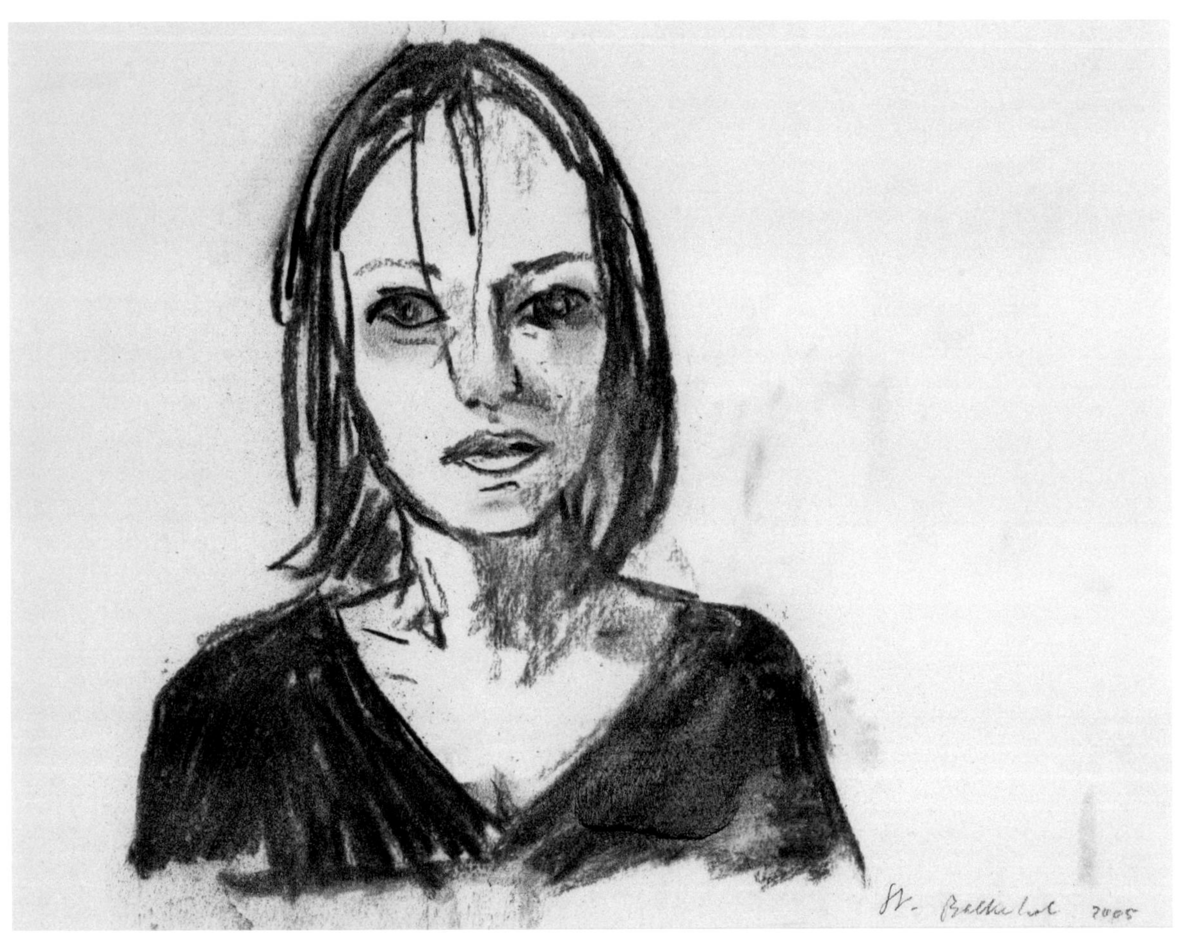

Untitled, 2005
charcoal on paper
17 x 21 inches
Collection of Renée and Paul Mansheim
Courtesy of Galeria Pepe Cobo, Madrid, Spain

Untitled, 2005
charcoal on paper
21 x 17 inches
Collection of Renée and Paul Mansheim
Courtesy of Galeria Pepe Cobo, Madrid, Spain

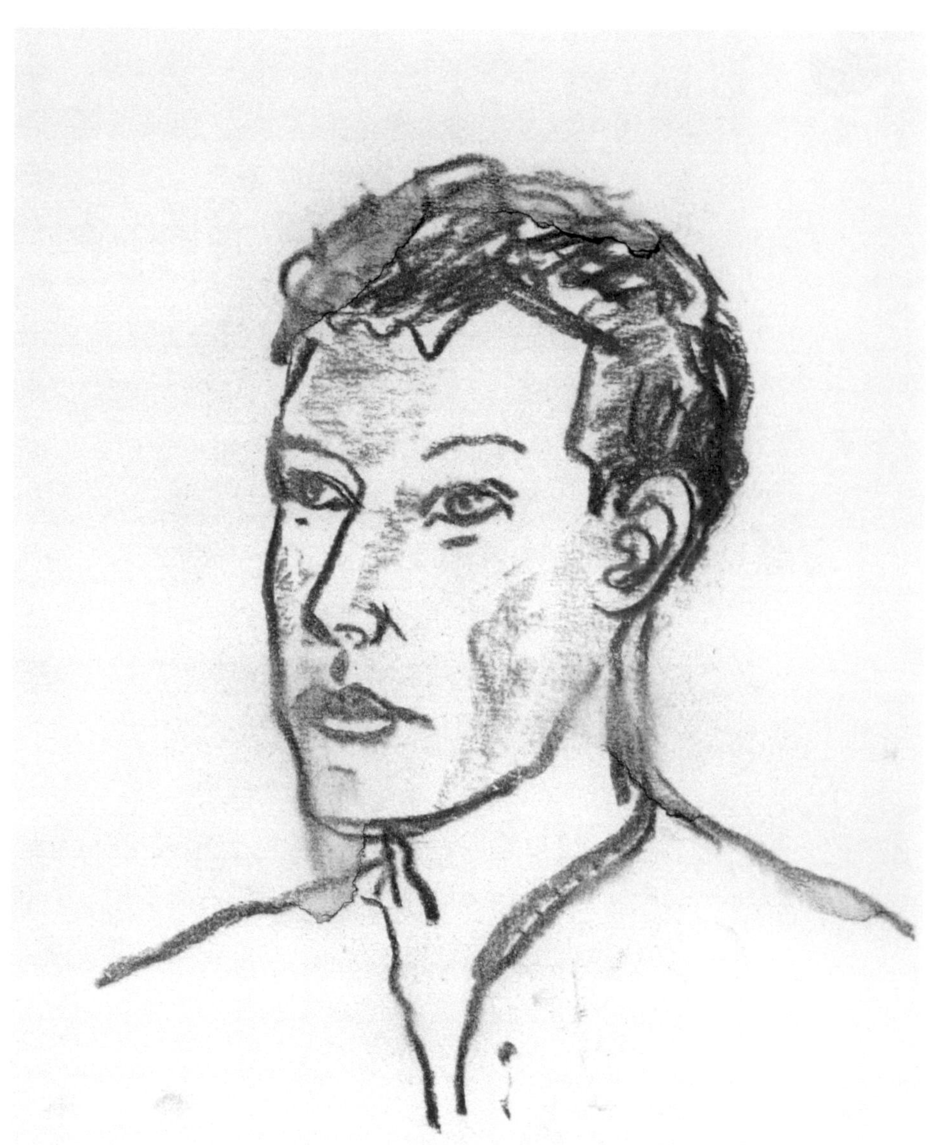

Stephen Barkalow 2005

Romare BEARDEN American, 1911-1988

Romare Bearden cited "the beauty of black woman" as a subject of immense importance, providing over a number of years one of his abiding motifs. While the persona may vary from nude, muse, lover, mother, grandmother, healer and friend, this figure is consistently and reverently assigned primary status. *Blue Nude* depicts a woman in a verdant garden, a wilderness that seems to be a sacred space. Integrated within this Edenic environment, the sensuous figure is auspiciously surrounded by birds and lush blossoms.

Bearden is a master of the improvisational medium of collage, a technique that enabled him to combine visual fragments from catalogs, magazines and books to create a compositional whole. While this collage may bring to mind Paul Gauguin's 19th century depictions of island women, it differs radically in intent. Rather than being a celebration of exoticism, Bearden's 20th century nude eloquently conveys the regal, mysterious and inviolable qualities of a beautiful black woman. C M H

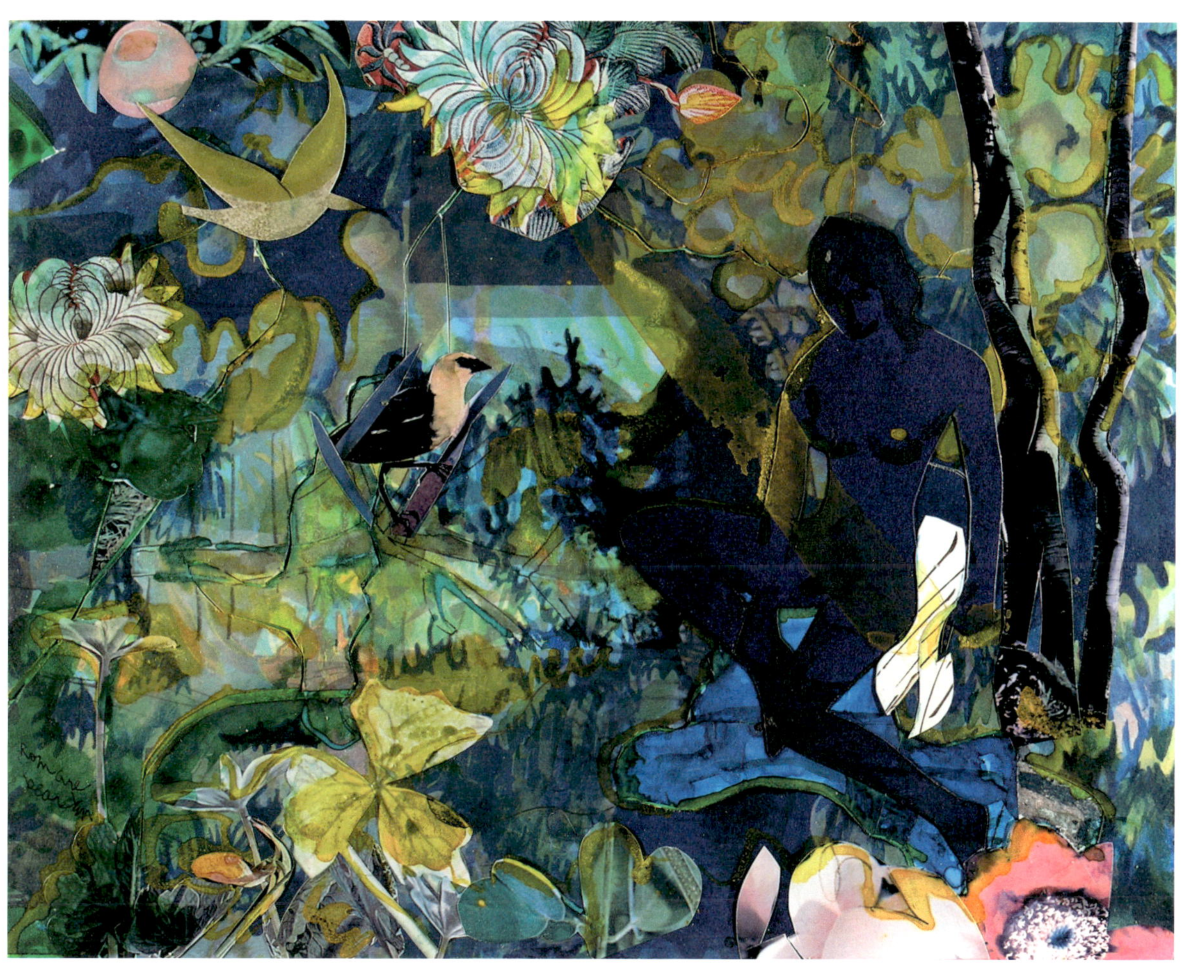

Blue Nude, 1981
collage and mixed media on board
14 x 18 inches
Collection of Jancy and Gilbert Patrick, North Carolina
Courtesy of Jerald Melberg Gallery

Carole BENZAKEN French, born 1964

Carol Benzaken utilizes photography, film and images from the media to investigate how representations of our surroundings are mediated through technology. *By Night*, a painting of a congested urban street, offers a disorientating perspective as oncoming headlights and ensuing darkness challenge one's ability to see clearly. Letters in the foreground seem to signify a pedestrian crossing, though crossing this particular street would be done with peril.

Using a photograph for reference, Benzaken intentionally removed much of the photographic detail as she created this expansive painting so that color and form would be the means by which the viewer would optically recognize its content. The scale of the painting is important because it more closely mimics one's actual experience of the urban landscape. Benzaken is interested in how we readily decipher codes and symbols, and how our perception is affected by viewing "reality" through the lenses of technology— the computer or TV monitor or cinema screen. "These different layers are changing our perception of reality, consciously or unconsciously…it is an alteration of reality," she says. C M H

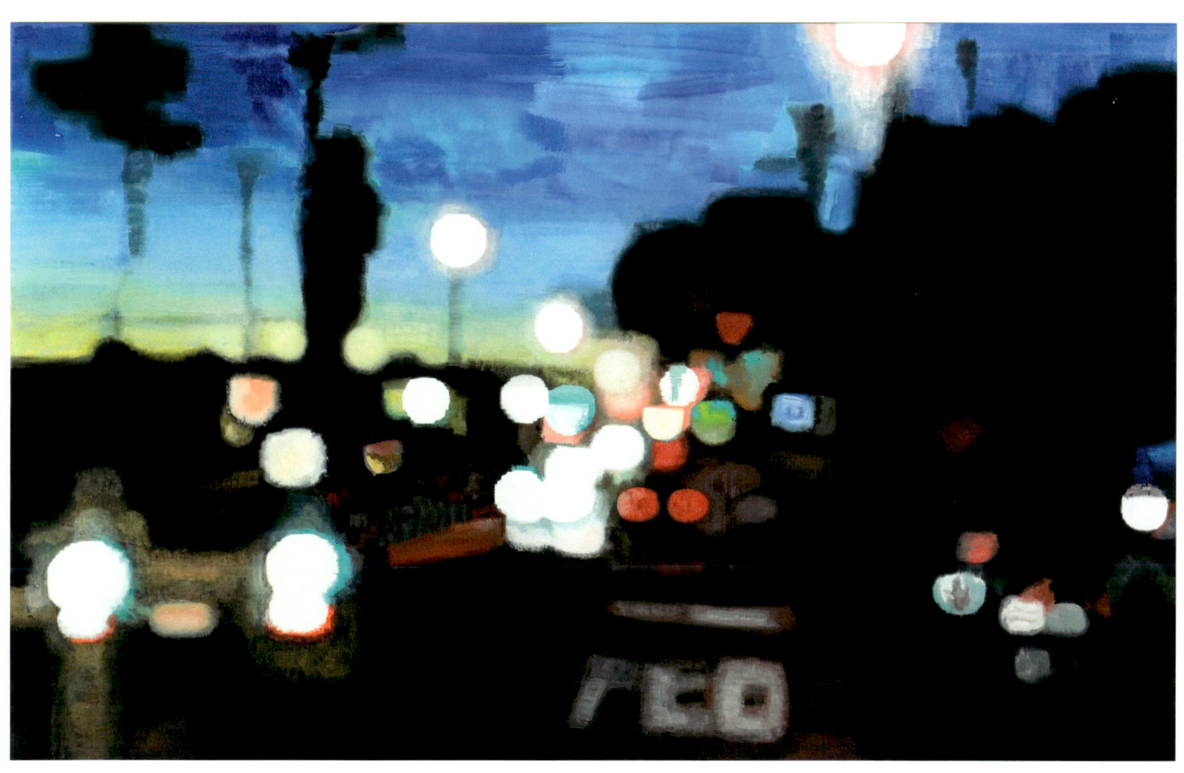

By Night, 2003
oil on canvas
89 x 124 inches
Collection of Adrián R. Halpern

Janet BIGGS American, born 1959

Janet Biggs turned from painting and sculpture to video installation in the 1990s, and has since become known for her focus on the performance of gender roles. Biggs plucks the threads of post-feminist discourse: she explores desire, identity, coming of age, discipline and athleticism in single- and multi-channel videos and multi-discipline performances. In *Airs Above the Ground*, Biggs combines footage of 14-year-old synchronized swimmer Deanna DeSimone with music composed and performed by cellist William Martina and drummer Blake Fleming. By inverting the recording of the already-inverted underwater ballet, she twice flips the perspective, adding to the sense of disorientation. Paralleling the social norms of adolescence, the swimmer attempts to perform motions that are graceful while simultaneously masking the strength and control required to appear so. Biggs's use of slow motion heightens the viewer's awareness of these qualities, inviting contemplation on masquerade and social performance. E B

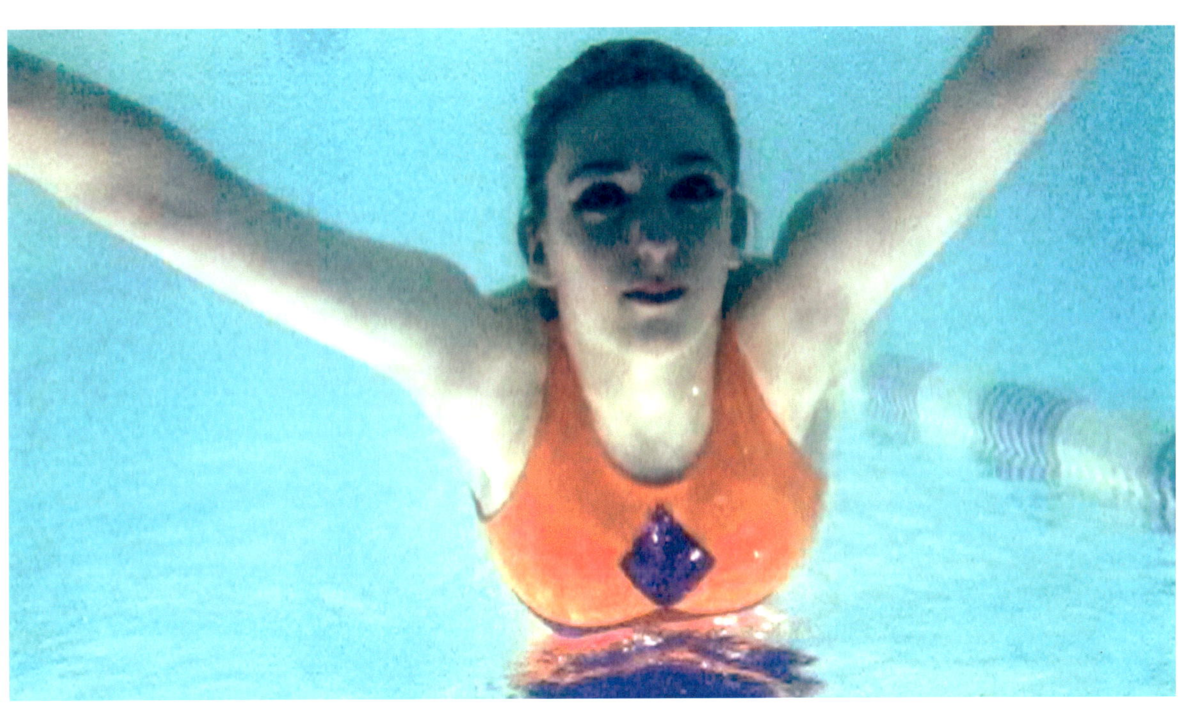

Airs Above the Ground, 2007
single-channel video (5.22 minutes)
photographed and directed by Janet Biggs,
music by William Martina and Blake Fleming
Collection of Dana and Rick Davis
Exhibition copy: Courtesy of Claire Oliver Gallery

Jeff BROUWS American, born 1955

Jeff Brouws, a California native, chronicles the decline of industrial small-town America in his photography while both exalting and critiquing the disappearing culture. He is noted for his unpopulated scenes of the American vernacular, scenes that he calls reflections of "abandonment and loss." Brouws endows his eerie nocturnal scenes of forgotten gas stations and back roads with vivid splashes of color. In *Mobil/Trailer, Inyokern, California*, for example, Brouws enlivens the filling station by enhancing the neon sign, rendering the building into an iconic beacon within the darkened Western landscape. Similarly, the single patch of light in *Playland, Rye, New York* draws attention to the carnival's darkened live reptile tent and evokes connotations of childhood, summer and carefree days left behind. Simultaneously mourning the abandonment of these institutions while revealing their character, Brouws' evocative photographs encompass the theater of the absurd, found art, and sharp portraiture. E B

Mobil/Trailer, Inyokern, California,
Highway 395, 1991
chromogenic dye coupler print (edition 1/5)
40 x 40 inches
Anonymous lender
Courtesy of the Artist and Robert Mann Gallery, New York

Playland, Rye, New York, 1990
chromogenic dye coupler print (edition 1/5)
40 x 40 inches
Anonymous lender
Courtesy of the Artist and Robert Mann Gallery, New York

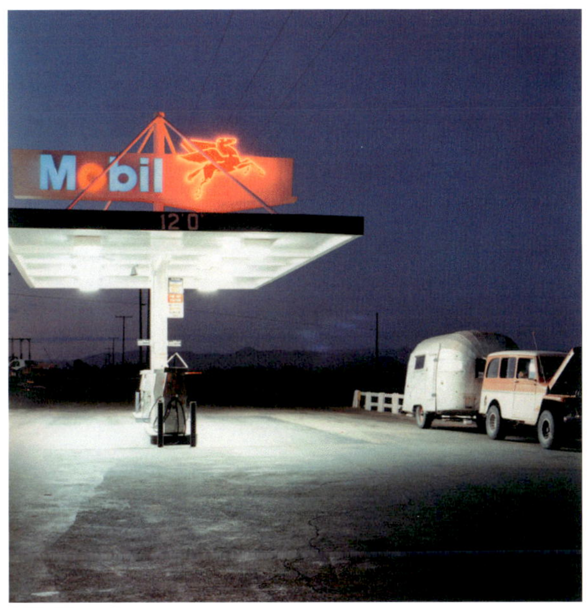

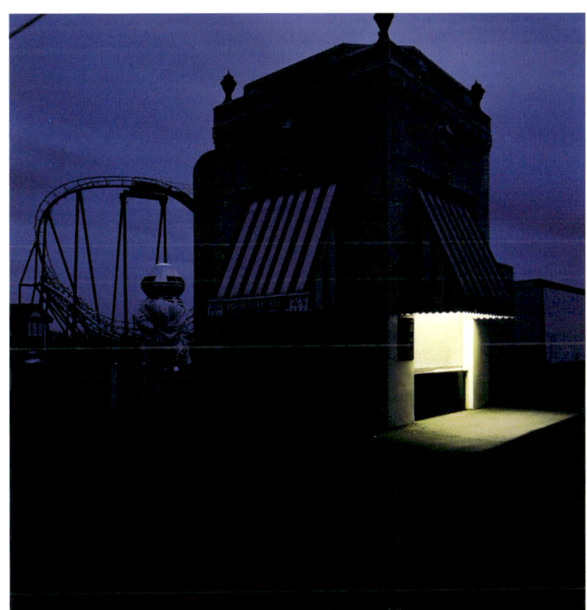

Edward BURTYNSKY Canadian, born 1955

These two photographs by Edward Burtynsky demonstrate man's impact upon his surroundings. Burtynsky's work instills the viewer with a sense of awe at what man has created as well as how human intervention has impacted the natural world. This sense of awe gives way to the distressing realization of the irreparable devastation of the land. Burtynsky's expansive landscapes seemingly reference the sublime, a theme also explored by many 19th century American landscape painters including Thomas Cole, Frederic Church and Jasper Cropsey. While these painters celebrated the vastness of the untrammeled American landscape, their paintings were often cautionary statements against the impending devastation that would be ushered in by industrialization and Western expansion.

Man's touch is evident within each of Burtynsky's photographs. *Rock of Ages #8, Abandoned Section, Wells-Lamson Quarry, Barre, VT* reveals how man has altered the earth by carving into it and by building on it. The rocks have been left in unnatural formations due to man's intervention, and one can see the massive cavern that has been carved out by humankind. In *Shipbreaking #27, Chittagong, Bangladesh* metal structures—remnants of ships—tower over the land, while tiny, barely visible figures use ropes to pry apart the massive detritus. S R

Rock of Ages #8, Abandoned Section,
Wells-Lamson Quarry, Barre, VT, 1991
chromogenic print (edition 3/5)
40 x 50 inches
Anonymous lender

Shipbreaking #27, Chittagong,
Bangladesh, 2001
chromogenic print (edition 4/5)
39 x 50 inches
Anonymous lender

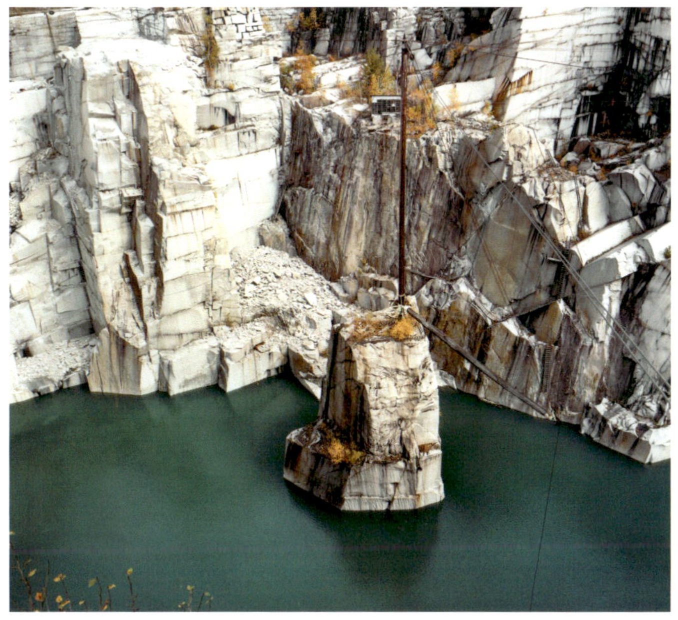

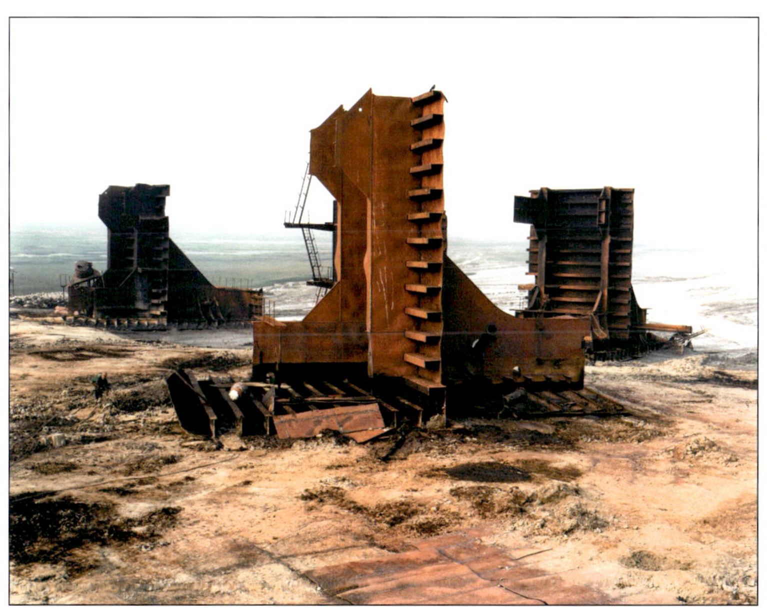

Sir Anthony CARO British, born 1924

Sir Anthony Caro continues the rich sculptural tradition of David Smith and Julio Gonzalez—pioneers who welded found steel objects to create abstract sculptures. In 1959, while still a student at London's Royal Academy, Caro began creating assemblages through welding. He befriended Kenneth Noland when he visited America in the late 1950s, and was inspired to use circular motifs that are prevalent in Noland's paintings. Noland, who purchased the last consignment of steel parts belonging to David Smith after his death in 1965, shipped the 37 tons of material to Caro in London, enabling Caro to effectively continue his sculptural explorations.

Over the course of his long and productive career, Caro has continued to stretch the limits of sculpture, going beyond the formalist preoccupation with internal relations. Caro has also addressed the problems inherent in effectively presenting smaller scale works on pedestals, arguing that to do so separated the sculpture from the "real world" and often implied that they were merely maquettes for larger works. Caro masterfully devised a solution with the creation of his *Table Sculptures* (1966-1969) which incorporated recognizable objects such as scissors and funnels, thereby establishing a real scale relating to the human hand. The intimately-scaled *Campanella* seems to reference Caro's earlier concerns with creating a more "real" sculpture that is appropriately scaled to its surroundings. C M H

34

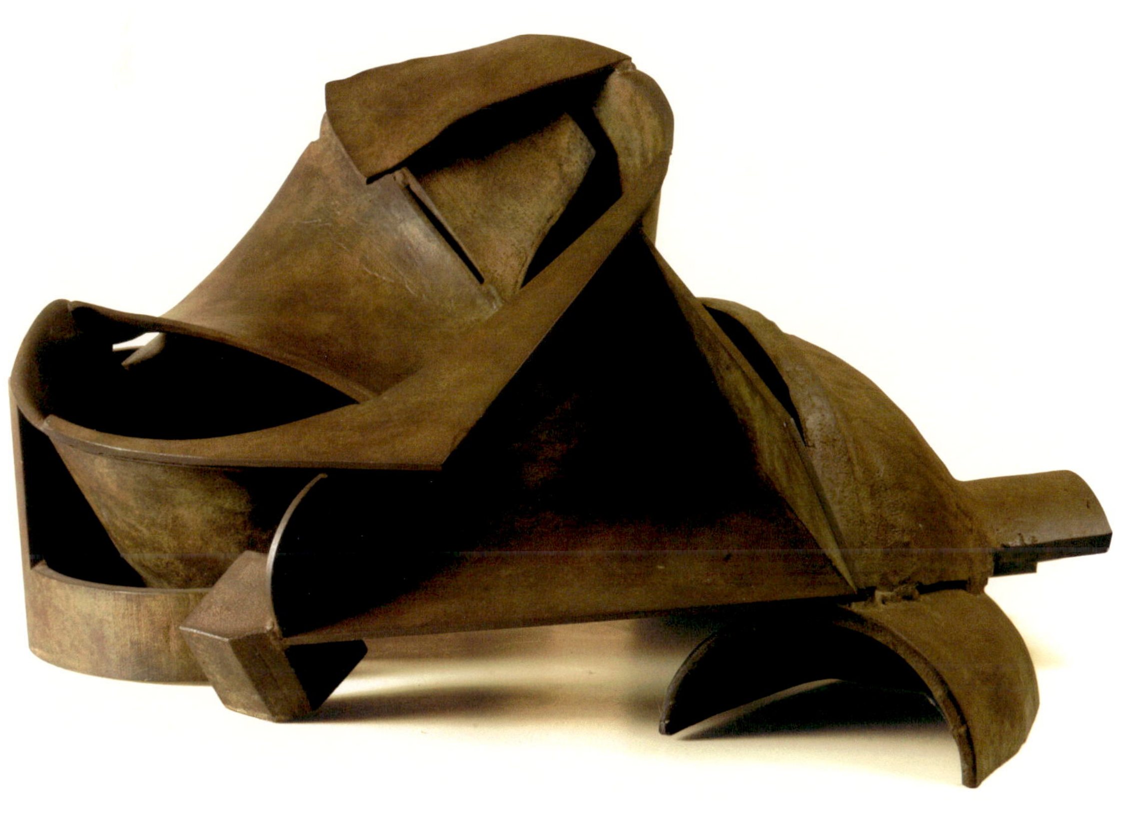

Campanella, 1983
brass and bronze cast and welded
16 ½ x 31 x 23 inches
Collection of Dr. J. Kenneth and Ellen T. Chance

35

Chuck CLOSE American, born 1940

While best known for his paintings, Chuck Close also creates prints of his iconic portraits and self-portraits. Early in his career Close's work was strikingly realistic. Gradually his approach has become more abstract, first by revealing the underlying grid and then by experimenting with colors and shapes within each of the squares of the grid, which effectively became compositions unto themselves.

The term "Ukiyo-e" now generally applies to water-based woodblock printing, but specifically it refers to Japanese-style woodcuts and paintings from the 17th to the 20th centuries that depict scenes from the pleasure quarters and from nature. When making a traditional Ukiyo-e style woodcut, one person draws on the blocks, makes color choices and prints the image while another person carves the blocks. Close's *Self-Portrait Woodcut* was made in collaboration with master printer Yasu Shibata, who both carved the woodblock and made color choices in consultation with Close. For *Self-Portrait Woodcut* approximately 46 blocks were carved and a separate color was applied to each block with a hand-made brush. As each block was printed in a designated order, the colors built upon and reacted with one another to create the final image. S R

Self-Portrait Woodcut, 2007
46-color handprinted Ukiyo-e style woodcut
on Shiramine paper (edition 25/60)
37 x 30 inches
Collection of Sonja and Isaac Luski
Courtesy of Pace Prints

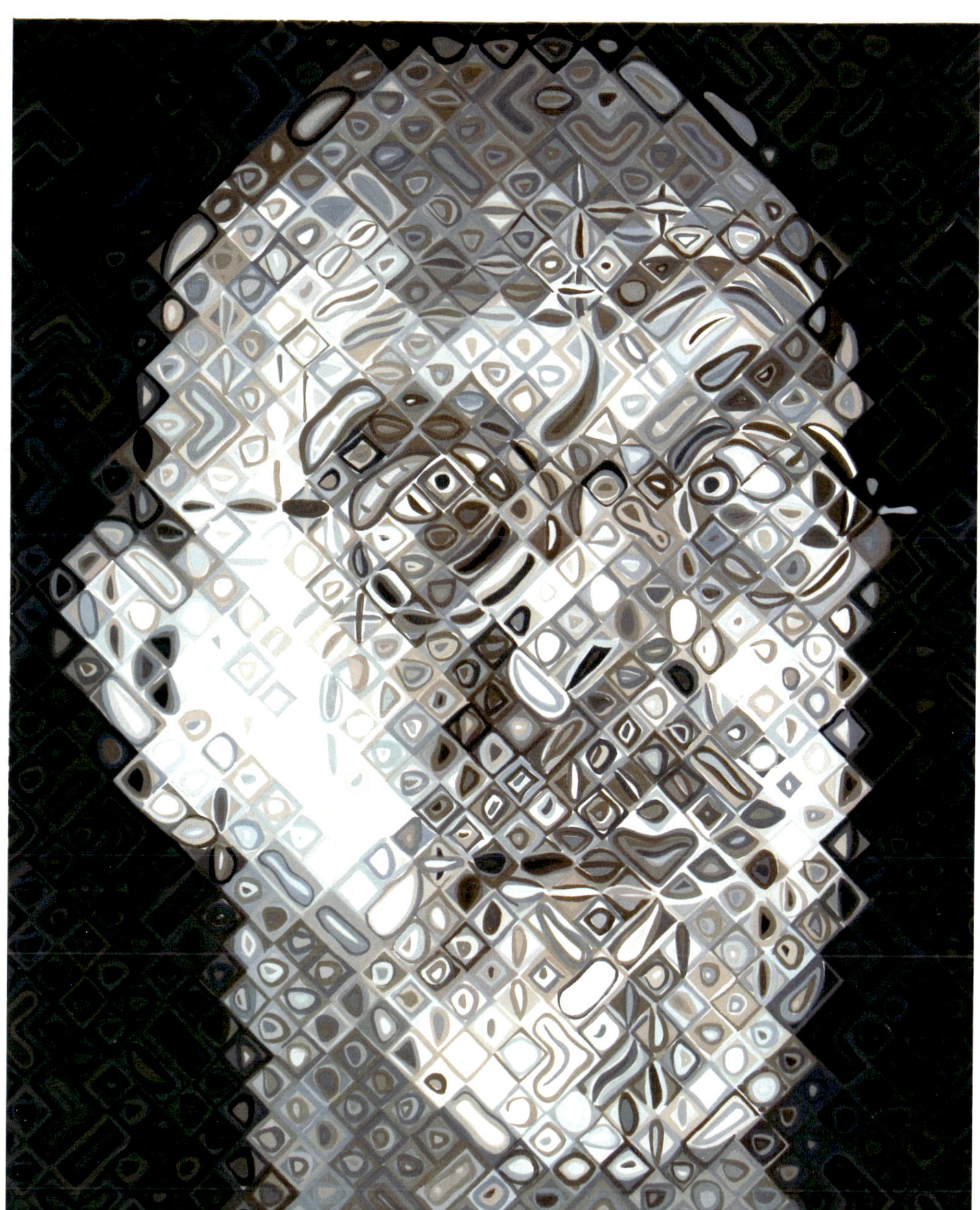

Gregory CREWDSON American, born 1962

Gregory Crewdson is one of several contemporary photographers who pioneered the practice of constructing and then photographing fictional realities. By creating a scene rather than shooting directly from the world around them, these photographers become the masters of their own reality and are able to control virtually every aspect of the photograph. The creation of each image becomes almost as complex and involved as a movie set. Crewdson works with his own lighting specialist and cooperates with town police to have roads or parks closed. His photographs have an affinity for science fiction films and their historical predecessors. This photograph, from his series entitled *Twilight*, focuses on suburban oddities and surreal occurrences. Most scenes are nocturnal, but contain an unearthly beam of light projected from an unseen source. In *Untitled* (pregnant woman/pool), the light hits the woman's enlarged belly, casting her as an eerie focal point. While contained in the picture, both the man at the base of the pool and the man reclining in the background seem emotionally unattached to her and unaware of the light enveloping her, as if they exist on a different plane of reality. L B

Untitled (pregnant woman/pool), 1999
laser direct chromogenic print (Ed: 10 PP)
50 x 60 inches
Private Collection, Dr. W. Kent Davis, Raleigh, North Carolina
Courtesy of the Artist and Luhring Augustine, New York

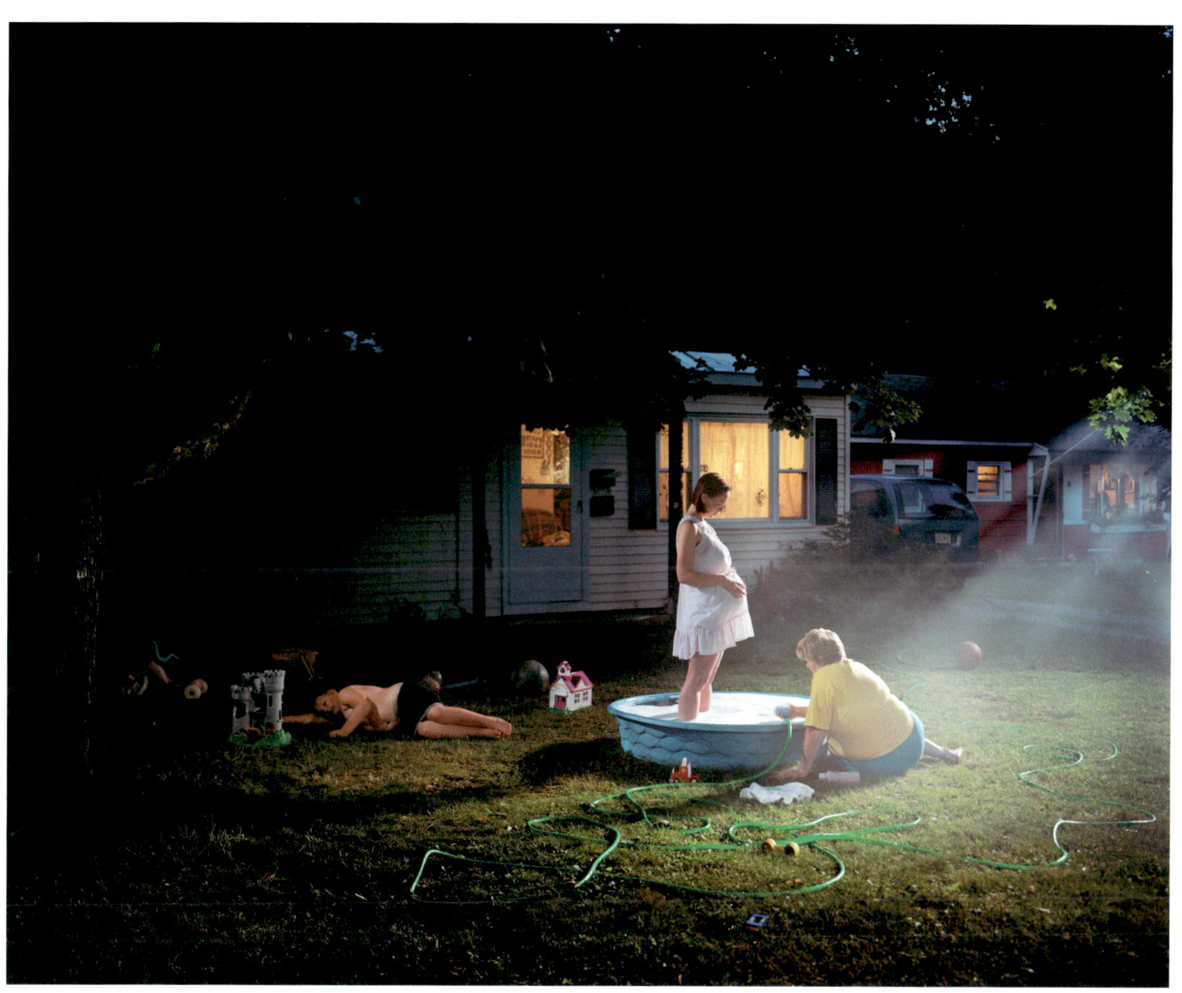

Willem de KOONING American, 1904-1997

Willem de Kooning was born in Rotterdam but became one of the leaders of the major American artistic movements of the 20th century. Known for constantly changing the rules of painting, de Kooning brought figurative representation and Abstract Expressionism together in the 1950s with his series of *Woman* paintings, executed with bold, energetic brushstrokes that radically abstract the subject of the painting.

In 1963 de Kooning moved to Long Island, New York, drawn to its proximity to water and the particular qualities of light that reminded him of his native Holland. His late paintings and prints, executed from the 1980s onward, are not so much landscapes but rather evocations of the artist's reaction to a particular place—its golden light and dappled reflections on water. While drawing has always been important to de Kooning, it is especially apparent in his later works where it appears as line as well as form. In *Quatre Lithographies*, one can see de Kooning's carefully controlled balance of color against a white background which imbues the prints with a transcendent quality. Although the lines are calm and reductive, there is still a sense of spontaneity that is the hallmark of Abstract Expressionist art. C M H

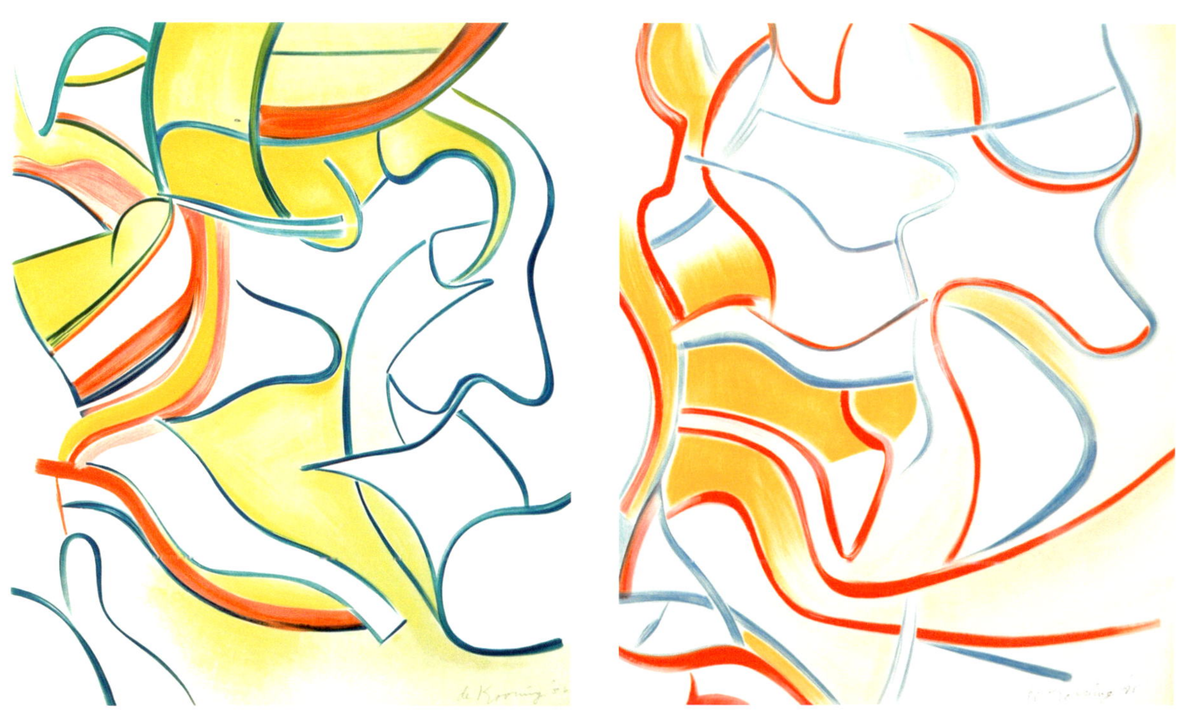

***Quatre Lithographies (Untitled II** and **Untitled III)**, 1986
lithograph (edition 72/100)
28 ¼ x 24 ¾ inches
Collection of Emily and Zach Smith

Richard DIEBENKORN American, 1922-1993

Richard Diebenkorn spent the bulk of his life and career in California. His paintings and prints contain many coastal allusions to the sky, seaside and bleached architecture of the area where he resided. He is widely recognized for his luminous *Ocean Park* series, which he began in 1967. These large-scale abstractions are not literal representations of the area that Diebenkorn traversed on a daily basis, but reveal his mastery at creating metaphorical explorations of color and space.

Diebenkorn was introduced to the work of Edward Hopper while he was a student at Stanford University and became enamored with "his use of light and shade and atmosphere…and its kind of austerity." It is apparent that Hopper's sensitivity to light and emotional resonance had an abiding effect on Diebenkorn. In both his abstract and figurative works, Diebenkorn masterfully balances an illusion of spatial depth and structure with its dissolution into light and space. His paintings abound with visible overpainting and reworking, but these traces of the artwork's evolution lend immediacy to the compositions. *Blue Surround*, one of Diebenkorn's later prints, exemplifies his sensitivity to surface modulation and the impression of depth. C M H

Blue Surround, 1982
spitbite etching and aquatint (edition 4/35)
35 1/8 x 26 1/4 inches
Collection of Emily and Zach Smith

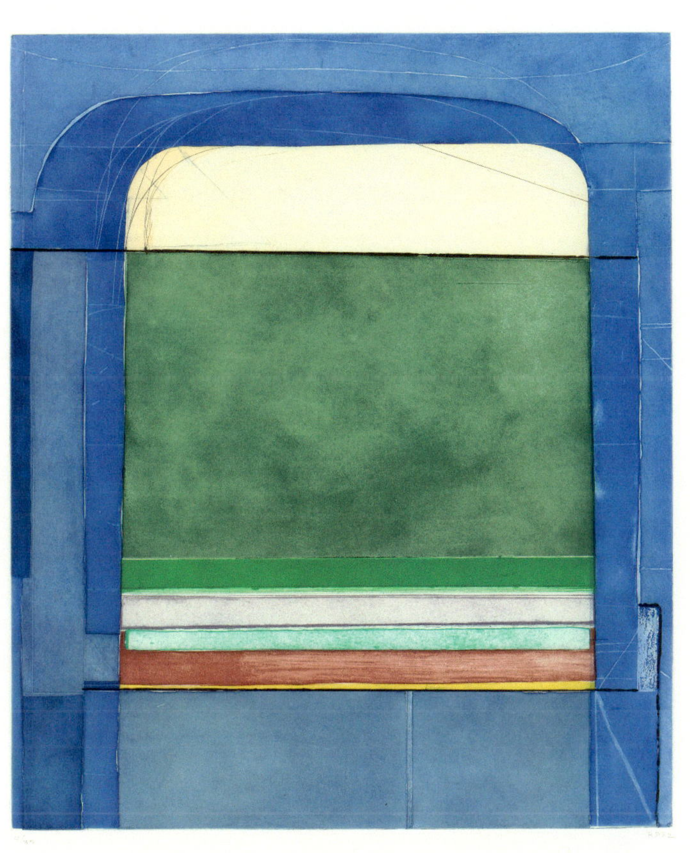

Tara DONOVAN American, born 1969

Tara Donovan constructs sculptures out of everyday objects, such as straws, plastic cups and toothpicks. Her work features reduced, simplified forms that emphasize both their own volume and scale and those of the places in which they are installed; it is therefore sometimes described as "Minimalist." Donovan's work is actually more in line with that of the Post-Minimalists, such as Eva Hesse, for it incorporates humble, everyday materials that are assembled in provocative new ways and that are clearly handmade by the artist rather than forged by a machine.

Controlled Caging, one of Donovan's earliest sculptures, is comprised of over 500,000 toothpicks held together by only friction and gravity. It is a tongue-in-cheek play on the fabricated metal sculptures made by Minimalist artists such as Donald Judd. Donovan's cube, however, is not a perfect, seamless form. Its structural integrity derives not from the fewest possible parts held together with welds or screws, but rather from the way in which natural forces act upon its thousands of individual parts. Donovan's cube also references landscapes and natural processes, as over a period of time entropy will occur as the cube's once clean edges are acted upon by gravity.
S R

Controlled Caging, 1996
wooden toothpicks held together entirely by friction and gravity
33 x 30 x 30 inches
Collection of Paul and Sara Monroe

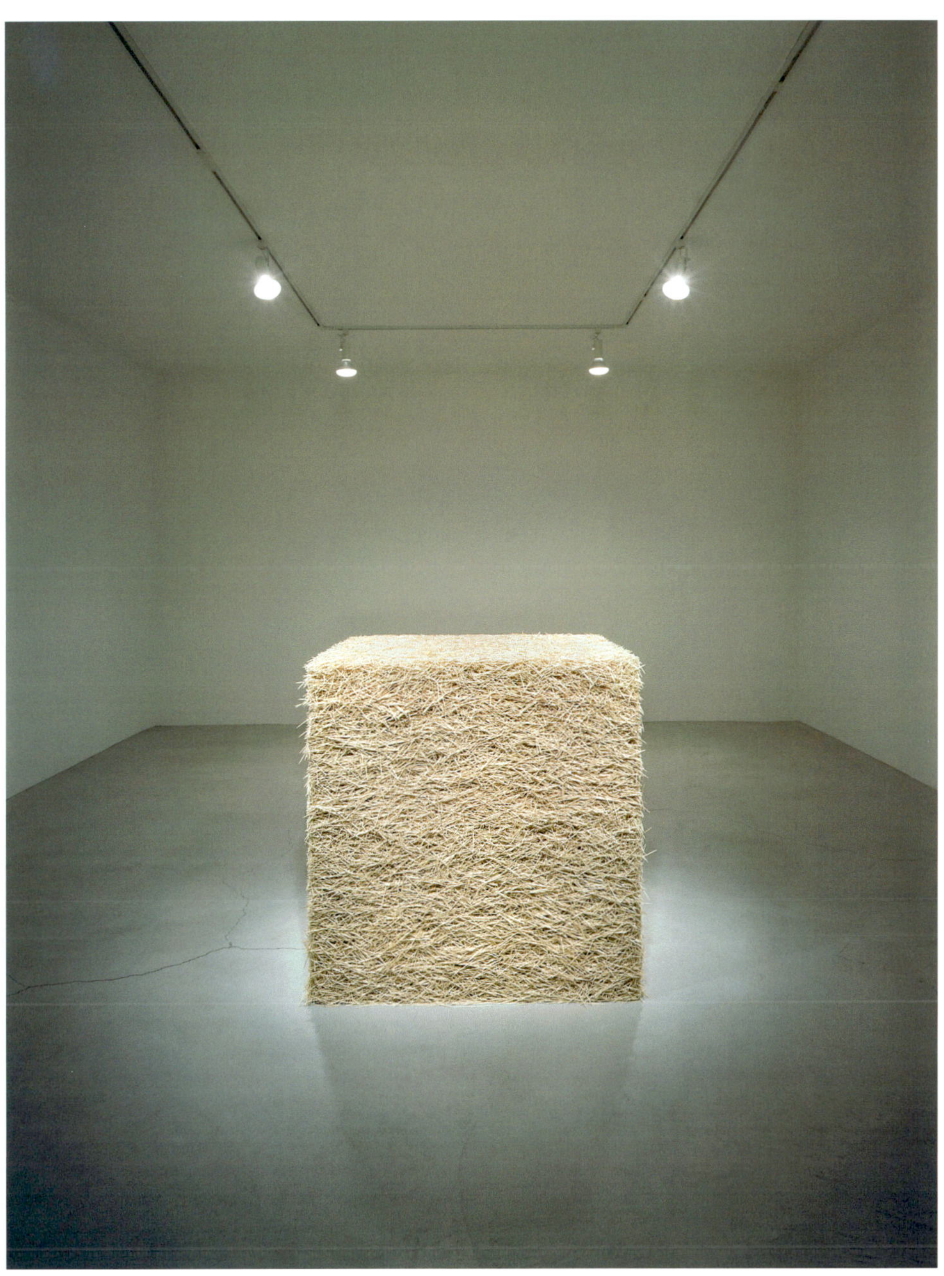

Michael EASTMAN American, born 1947

Michael Eastman travels America, Cuba and Europe in search of store fronts and old houses. He photographs these dilapidated buildings and works to tease out of them a sense of their former grandeur. He chooses dramatic angles in order to give his photographs a larger-than-life feel, and his carefully calculated compositions and sensitivity to color lend his work a painterly quality and an unmistakable elegance. While his photographs almost always lack people, there is typically an inference of human presence.

Green Interior, from his *Cuba* series, reveals Eastman's ability to capture fading interiors of decaying grandeur. There is no doubt that at one time this room was stylish and opulent, but the cracked moldings and damaged furniture reveal that it is clearly long past its prime. The complementary tones of the green walls and red furnishings create a quiet radiance. Eastman utilizes a careful balance of horizontal and vertical lines to create a compositional harmony within this photograph. S R

Green Interior, 2002
chromogenic print (edition 3/15)
47 x 35 inches
The Frank Konhaus and Ellen Cassilly Collection

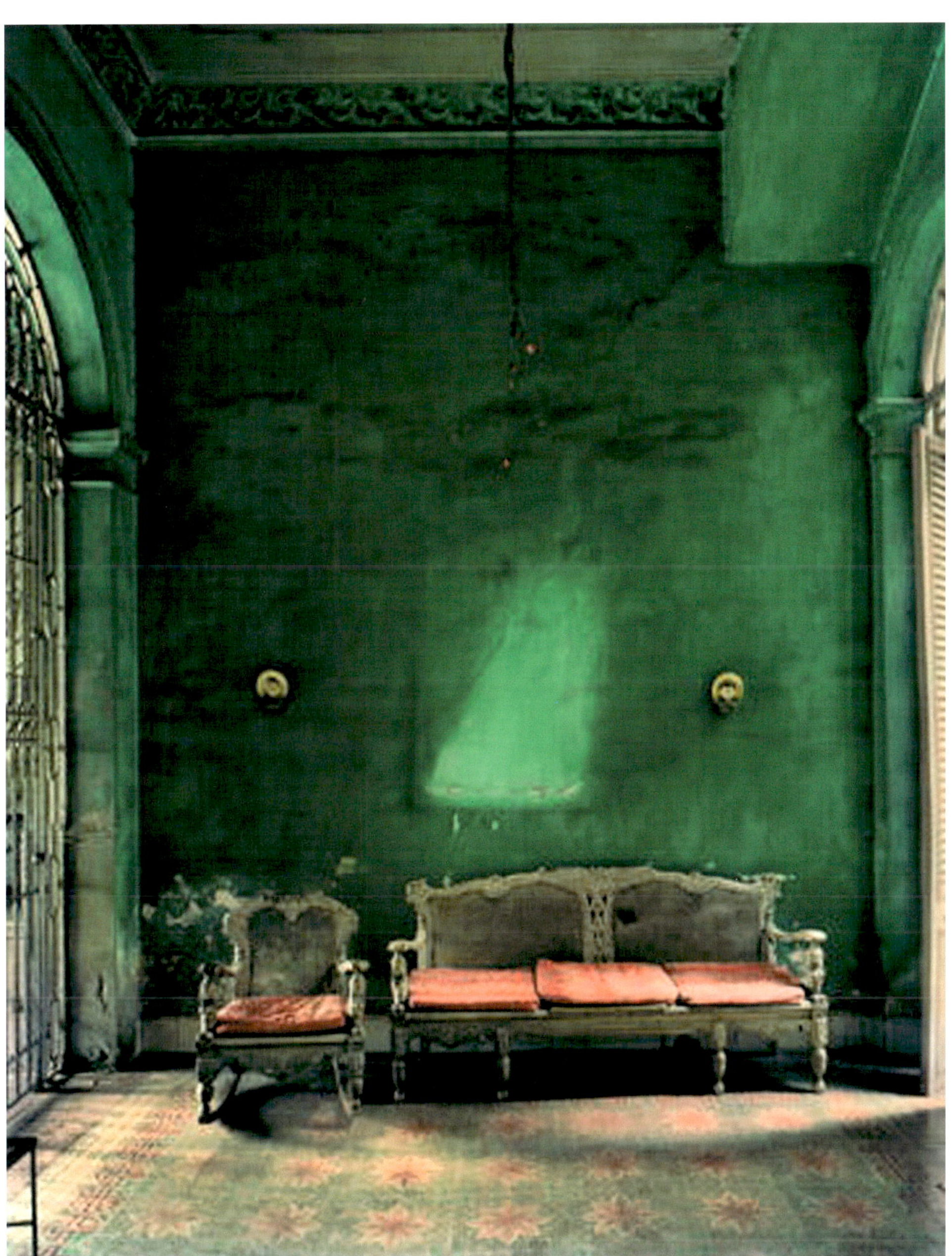

Lalla ESSAYDI Moroccan, born 1956

As a girl growing up in Marrakesh, Morocco, Lalla Essaydi was often banished to a palace owned by her family on the outskirts of the city. She, along with the other female members of her family, was sent there as punishment for wrongdoings, most of which were considered crimes only to Muslims. In her series *Converging Territories*, Essaydi returns to this house with female relatives and friends to reclaim the space as their own. Draped in fabric completely covered in hennaed calligraphy, a form of artistic writing illegal for women to learn, the subjects, whose bodies are also covered in calligraphy, stand face-on in front of canvas backdrops bearing hennaed writing. The words are taken from Essaydi's diary, and begin "I am writing. I am writing on me, I am writing on her," and continue, "I am dreaming about freedom and don't know how to talk about it." L B

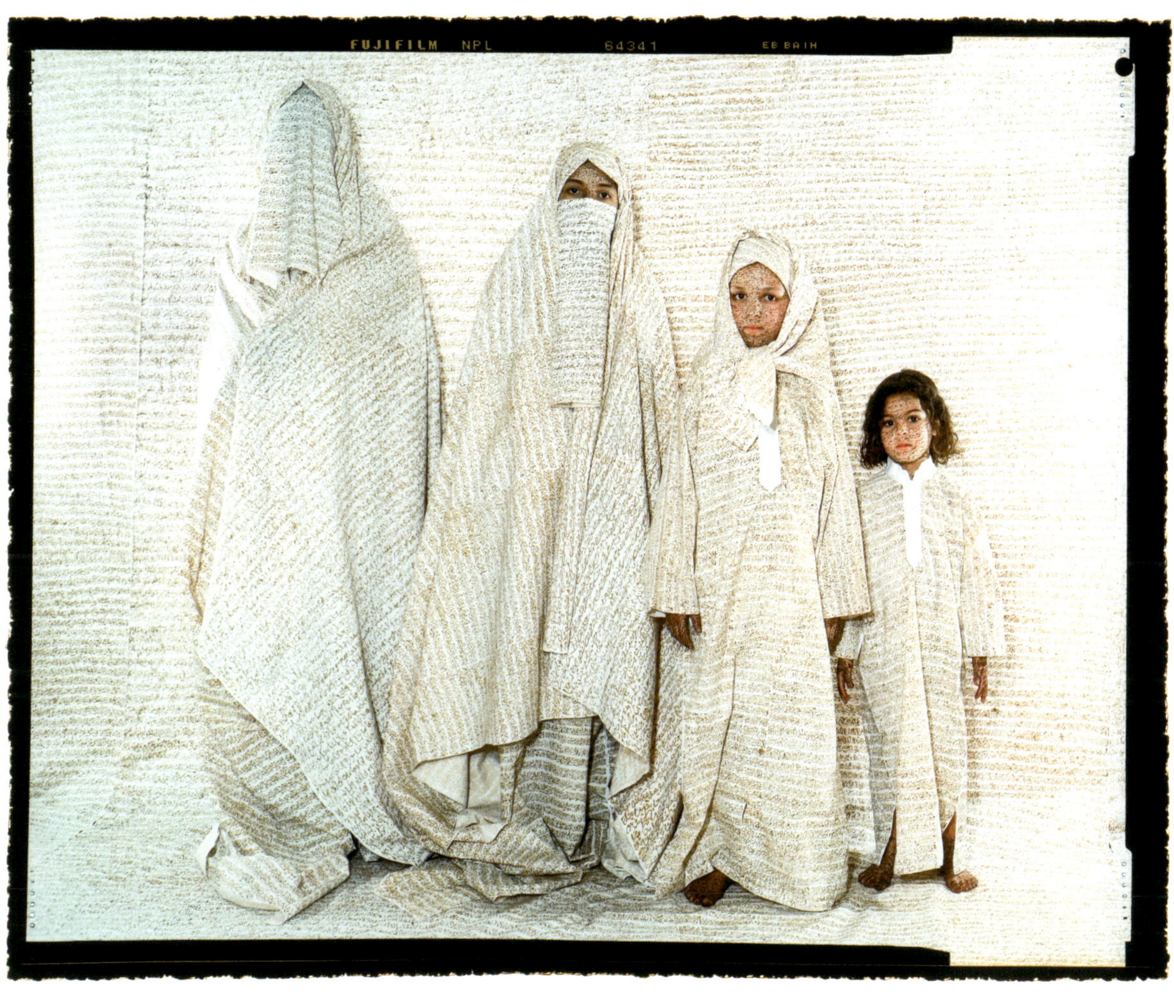

49

Converging Territories #7, 2004
chromogenic print (AP)
30 x 40 inches
Collection of Adrián R. Halpern

Sam FRANCIS **American, 1923-1994**

Born in California, Sam Francis experimented with a wide variety of painting styles ranging from Surrealism to Abstract Expressionism. Traveling extensively as a young artist, the time Francis spent in both Paris and Japan solidified his interest in portraying the ineffable qualities of light and color. By the 1950s Francis had developed a style that departed from the expressive iconography of the Abstract Expressionists and came to focus instead on the sensuous quality of color, as well as compositions that conveyed a "ceaseless instability."

Later in his career Francis' paintings and prints were characterized by a bold use of white space and asymmetrical compositions. *Meteorite*, a monumental print, reveals an explosive energy conveyed through the primary colors of red, yellow and blue. Drips, splatters, brilliant hues and arabesque lines imbue this screenprint with a celebratory, even hedonistic quality. CMH

50

Meteorite, 1986
screenprint (edition 11/65)
72 ¼ x 42 inches
Collection of Thomas E. Kanes and Susan Valentine Kanes

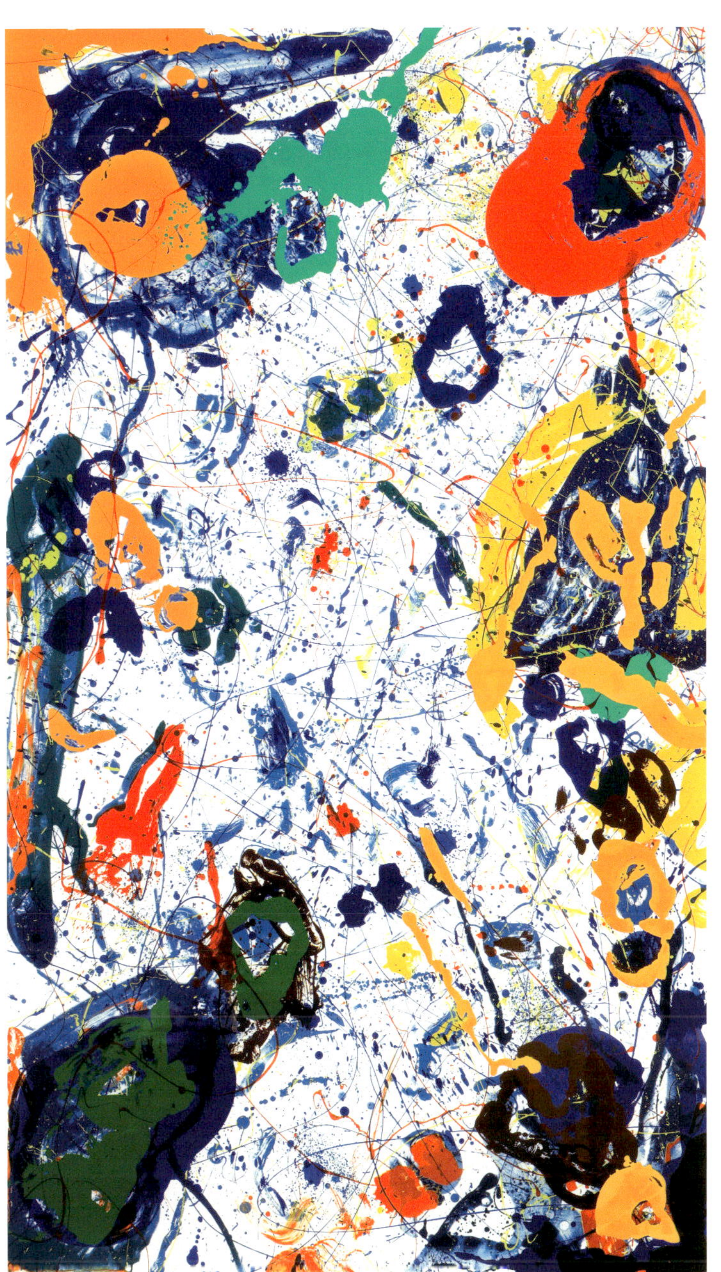

Helen FRANKENTHALER American, born 1928

Helen Frankenthaler is known for the innovative stained-canvas technique she helped pioneer in 1952. By pouring thinned paint directly onto unprimed canvas, allowing the weave of the fabric to remain visible, she created a closer relationship between image and surface, thereby drawing attention to both the material and the medium. Frankenthaler's earlier works contained many expressive lines, splashes and drips. By the late 1960s her paintings became more richly colored meditations that consciously explored large abstract forms as they related to the edge of the canvas. *Denominator* exemplifies Frankenthaler's dynamic arrangements of colors and shapes to create a harmonious spatial composition.

More intimately scaled, *The Fourth* reveals Frankenthaler's playful approach as she painted an exuberant pink form, inscribed the words "jump rope," and whimsically dotted the paper with red, white and blue splotches. There is a great deal of spontaneity and immediacy in this lyrical composition, which reveals Frankenthaler's mastery of drawing with color. C M H

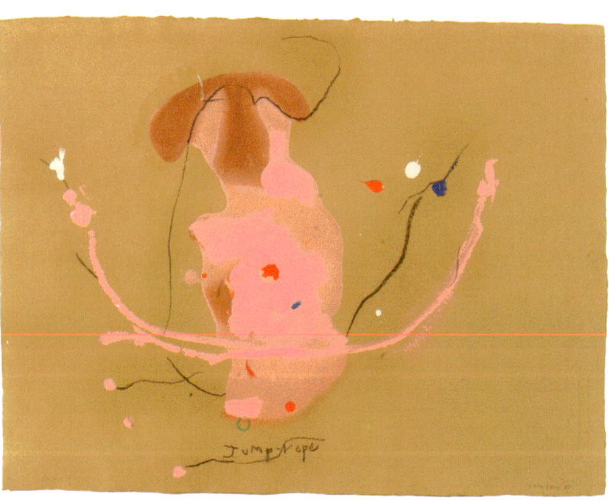

The Fourth, 1985
acrylic and charcoal on paper
20 ¼ x 26 ¼ inches
Collection of Dr. J. Kenneth
and Ellen T. Chance

Denominator, 1967
acrylic on canvas
104 x 69 inches
Collection of Dr. J. Kenneth
and Ellen T. Chance

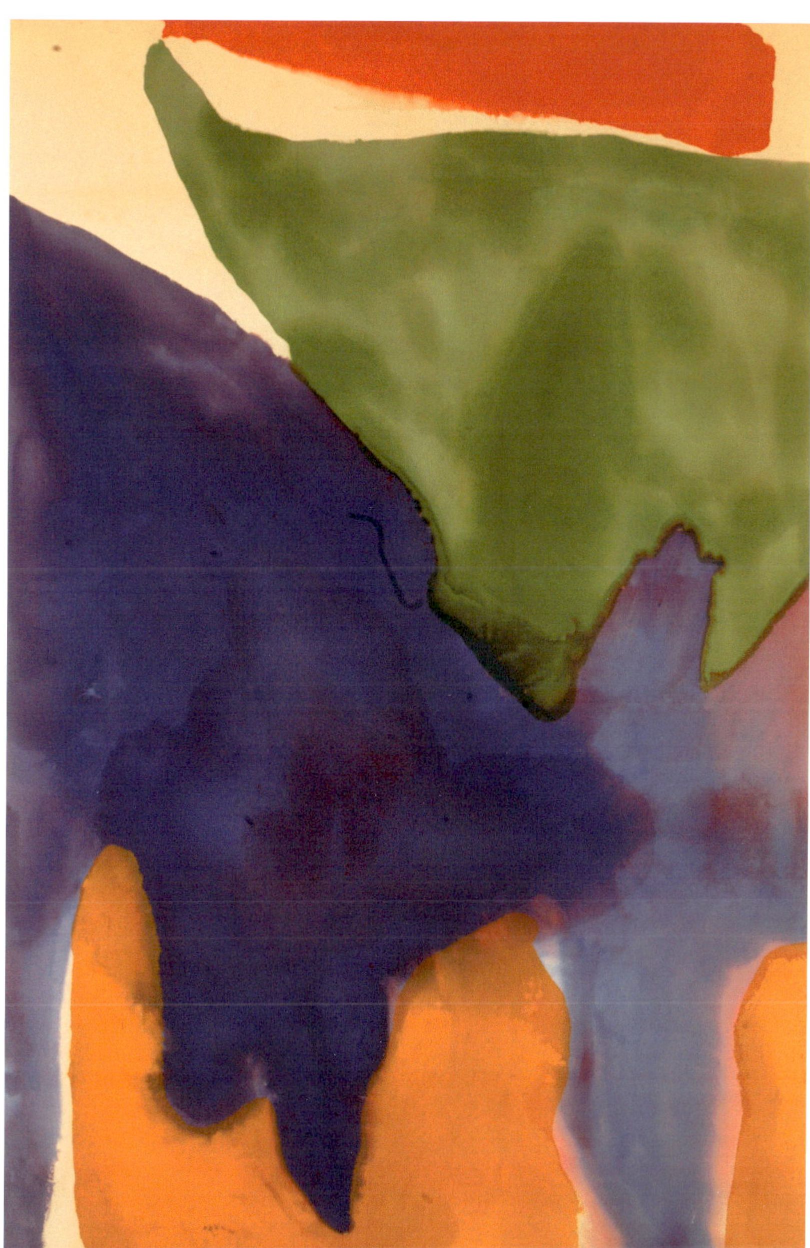

53

Eric Freeman's minimal compositions feature bars of graduated color that seem to shift and glow like neon lights. Part trompe l'oeil, part Op Art, these works bring depth and movement to the two-dimensional canvas through the use of bright, contrasting colors. Painstaking strokes of paint run parallel across the canvas, seeming to extend the painting into infinity. Although acknowledging influences from many sources, Freeman strives to distance his art from the self-conscious pop art of the previous generation, saying, "I want my work to be self-contained, from my own head." In *Turquoise Inside Yellow*, Freeman's use of not-quite complementary colors lends an additional tension to the pulsing piece. Here, as in his other works, the meticulous and structured application of paint yields to the illusion of free-flowing form, juxtaposing the process through which it was created with its ultimate effect on the viewer. E B

54

Turquoise Inside Yellow, 2006
30 x 30 inches
oil on linen
Collection of Ginger Kemp
Courtesy of Mary Boone Gallery, New York

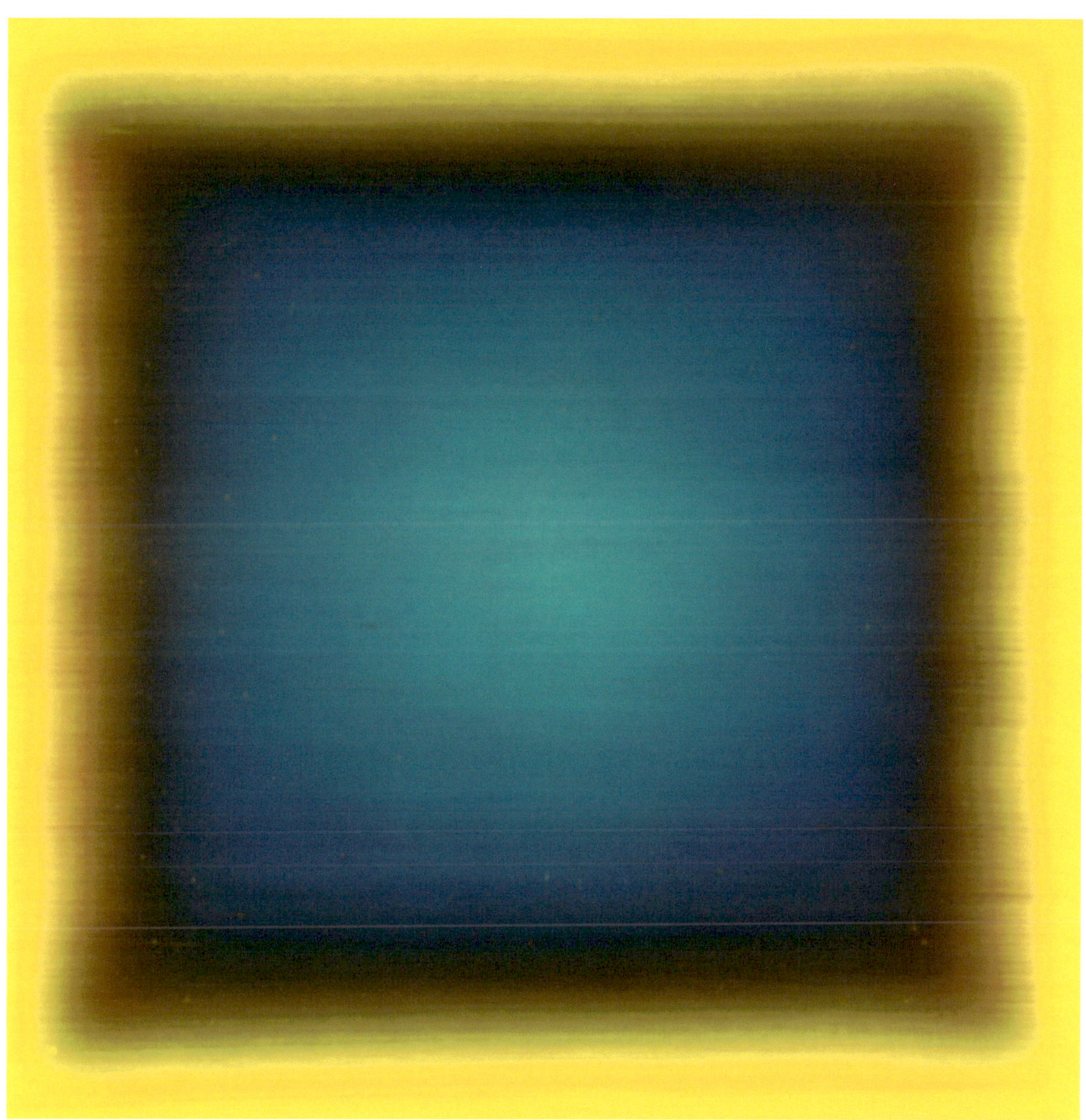

Wyatt GALLERY American, born 1975

Although there are no people in photographer Wyatt Gallery's series *After the Storm*, he considers it to be a collection of portraits. After the tsunami that occurred in Sri Lanka in 2004, Gallery was deeply distraught and journeyed with his camera to capture what he saw. His experiences so affected him that he continued to document natural disasters and found himself in New Orleans after Hurricane Katrina struck. Initially drawn to the mystery of the destruction, Gallery stayed because of the quiet beauty he found in the emptiness of the city. By photographing the objects that were left behind, he poignantly captures glimpses into individuals' lives as clearly as if their faces were depicted: "Through a Bible in a church, or a quilt on a bed," he writes, "the viewer is able to connect through similar objects and begin to understand what it must feel like to lose everything you own." LB

Alma, St. Rita's Nursing Home St. Bernard Parish LA, 2005
chromogenic print (edition 3/4)
30 x 38 inches
The Frank Konhaus and Ellen Cassilly Collection

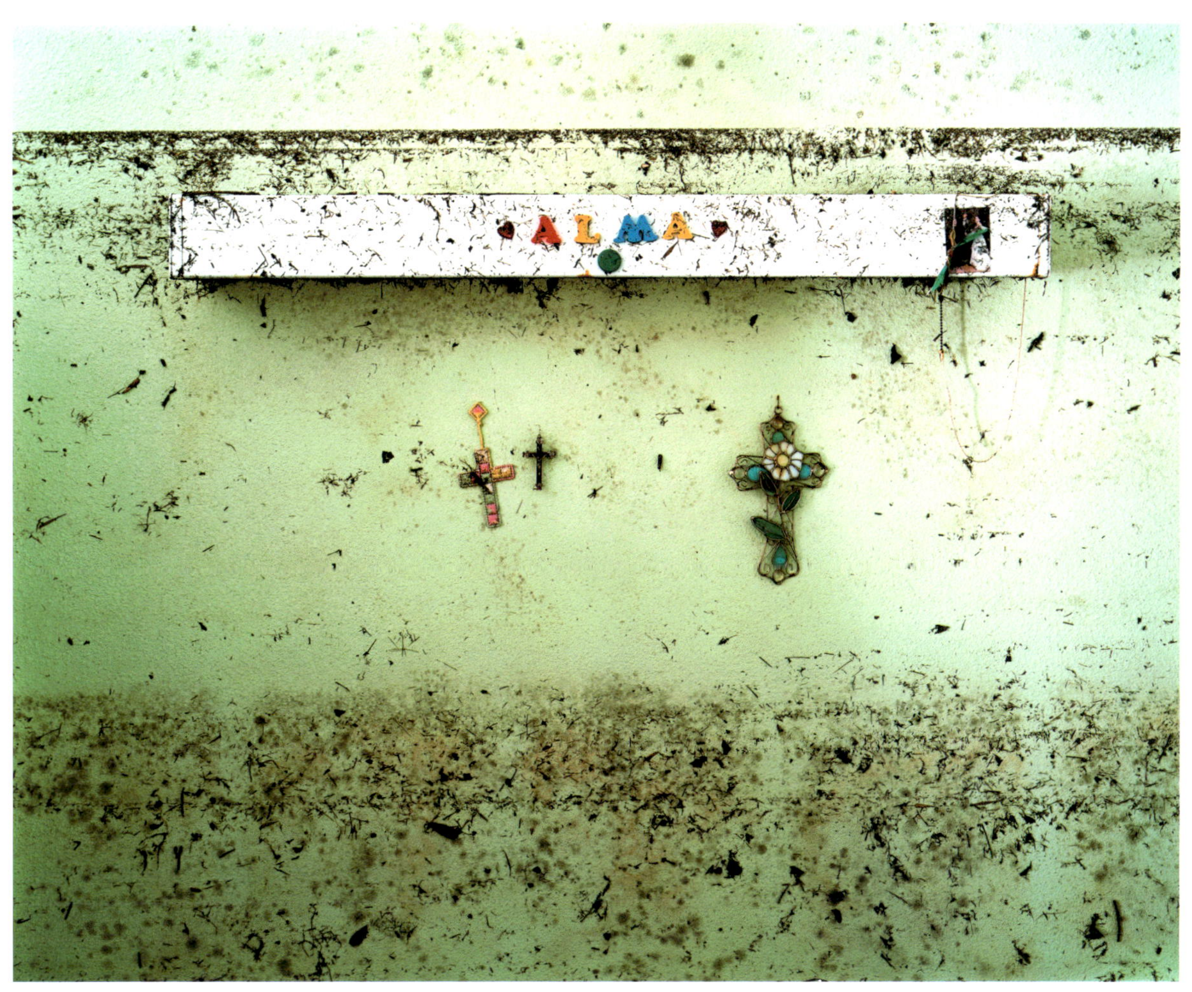
ALMA

Rimma **GERLOVINA** and Valeriy **GERLOVIN** Russian, born 1951, 1945

Growing up in the heavily-censored Soviet Union and leading an underground avant-garde artist collective forced the Russian couple Rimma Gerlovina and Valeriy Gerlovin to live in a world surrounded by double meanings and innuendos. Carrying the ideas that the past and future are contained in the present and that two bodies can occupy the same space at the same time, the Gerlovins have dubbed their work photoglyphs. Derived from two opposite Greek words, photo meaning "writing with light" and glyph meaning "carved symbol," the word aptly captures the sentiments expressed in their body of work. Inspired by religious icon painting, seen here in the suspension of Rimma's head in a black, nondescript background, their work often seems to aim to cause viewers to question and think about what is held to be true. In *Birth of Aphrodite,* Rimma's braided hair spirals around her, appearing as expanding water rings and creating an image in which the end and the beginning—birth and death—blend into one. L B

Birth of Aphrodite, 1992
Ektacolor c-print (edition 9/10)
41 ½ x 48 inches
The Frank Konhaus and Ellen Cassilly Collection

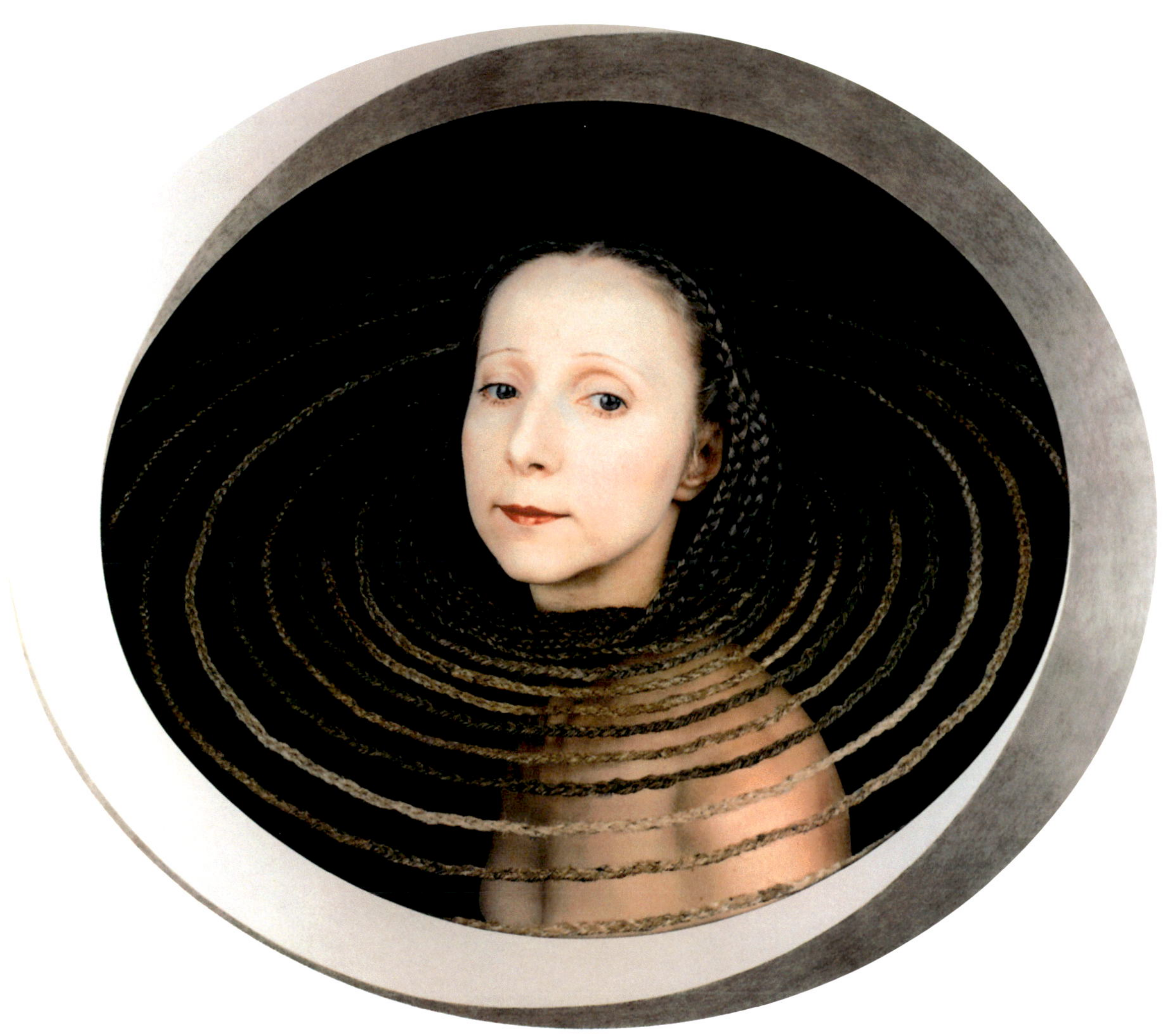

Robert GOBER American, born 1954

Robert Gober has gained an extensive reputation for his highly detailed sculptures, which almost always carry underlying political meanings. Hauntingly realistic, designed to be emotionally charged, the familiar objects he crafts, from drains and furniture to uncannily detailed body parts, explore the associations, memories and attachments the viewer has to certain inanimate items. *Untitled (shoe)*, Gober's red wax Mary Jane, conjures feelings of childhood innocence and fragility. The single shoe's existence, absent from its owner, eerily illuminates this temporary stage of life and speaks to the value of adolescence. The temporal nature of life is also addressed in *Newspaper (Hare Escobar.,/Wedding)*. A sappy wedding announcement, oozing with commercial romance, finds its home nestled in a newspaper telling of natural disasters and the imminent destruction of the world. However unsettling, Gober's work, as intended, blends perfectly into a domestic setting. Its ability to masquerade makes it even more haunting. L B

Untitled (shoe), 1990
red casting wax
3 x 2 ⁵/₈ x 7 ½ inches
Collection of Paul and Sara Monroe

Newspaper (Hare Escobar.,/Wedding), 1992
photolithograph on super fine Mohawk paper, twine (edition 5/10)
6 x 16 ¼ x 13 ¼ inches
Collection of Paul and Sara Monroe

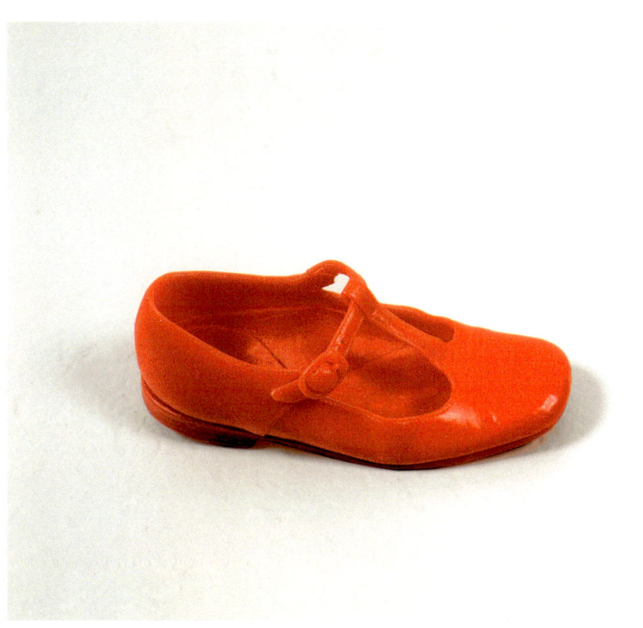

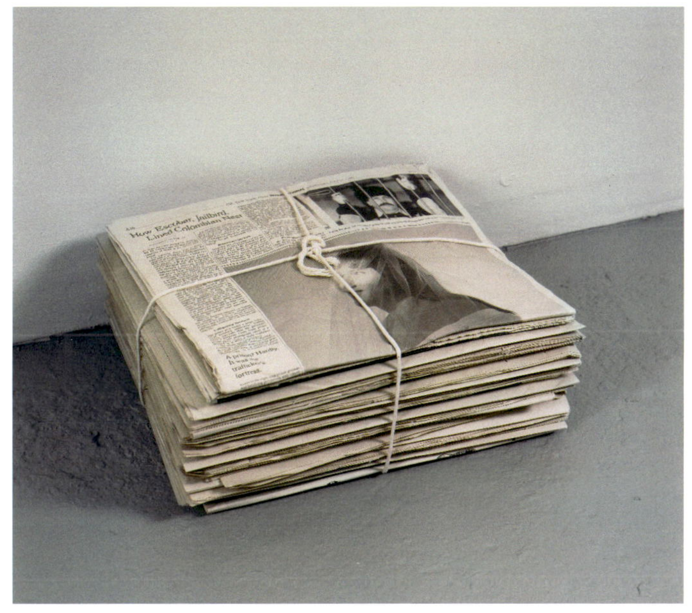

Anthony GOICOLEA American, born 1971

Photographer Anthony Goicolea is best known for his pseudo self-portraits, replacing the heads of boys in school uniforms or figures swimming in a pool with his own. Through this distortion of reality, Goicolea pushes the limits of identity and explores issues of age and gender, self-love and self-hate, discipline and impulse, technology and religion. In *Pool Pushers #2*, Goicolea has portrayed himself as the orderly onlooker of a scene that is perhaps both frightening and pathetic. Boys float twisted and facedown in a pool as they are poked with nets from above. In a dramatic switch from self-portraiture and the figure, *Smoke Stack* is from Goicolea's most recent show, "Almost Safe." Here he explores the future of a world ravaged by industrialization and capitalism over the last century. Similar to his earlier work, the scene elicits both fear and disgust, but also pity and empathy for what the world has become. L B

Pool Pushers #2, 2001
chromogenic print mounted on aluminum (edition 2/3)
71 x 108 inches
Private Collection, Dr. W. Kent Davis, Raleigh, North Carolina

Smoke Stack, 2007
black and white photograph mounted on aluminum and laminated with non-glare Plexiglas (edition 1/9)
55 x 60 inches
Collection of Allen Thomas, Jr., Wilson, North Carolina

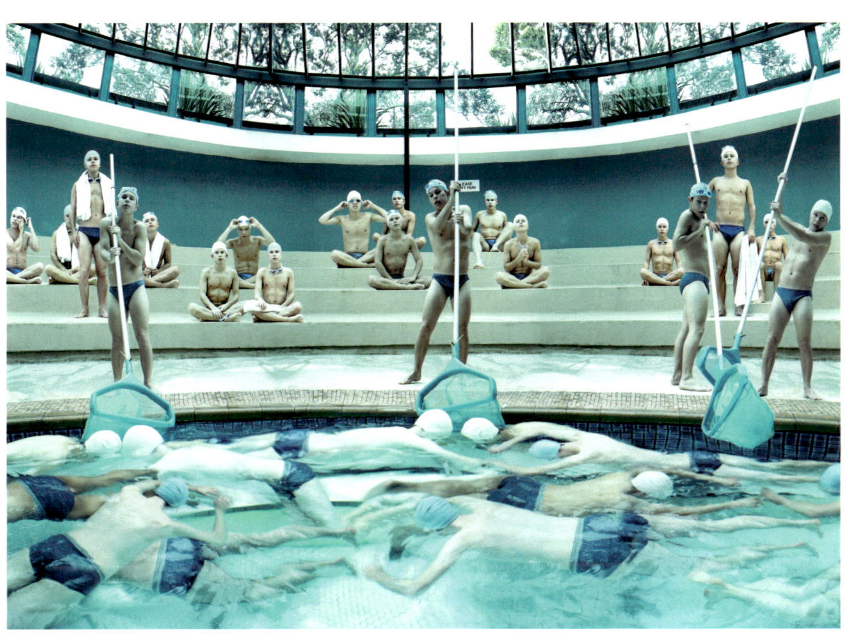

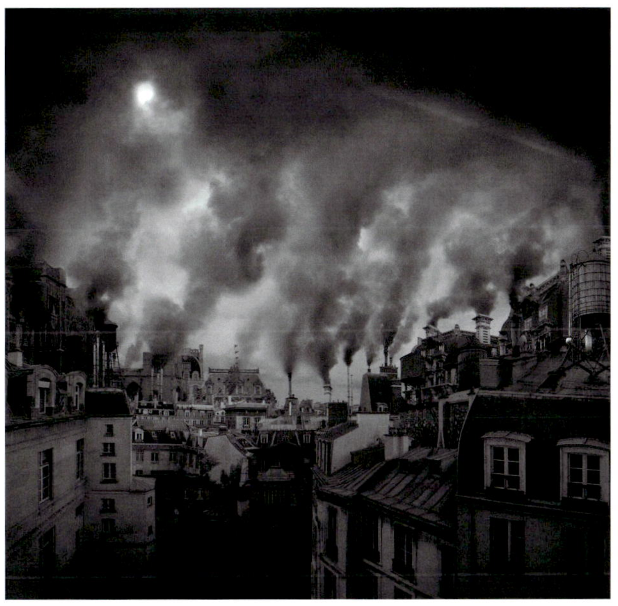

Andy **GOLDSWORTHY** British, born 1956

Andy Goldsworthy, an internationally recognized installation artist, began creating works within the landscape in the 1970s when concern for the environment reached a new height. Composed of natural materials found within the environment, most of his work is created outdoors and is site-specific. Goldsworthy utilizes leaves, rocks, sticks, earth and ice found in the immediate area to create his works, which are then acted upon by the weather and environment. He then photographs his sculptures because of the transient nature of his work; these photographs are often the only means to view his sculptural installations, which are often created in remote areas. His art references man's interaction with nature and how we often become removed from experiencing the natural world in an unmediated way.

This photograph documents flame-like forms that Goldsworthy carved into a block of snow, emphasizing the temporal quality of the sculpture which will soon be reclaimed by nature, as well as the paradox of the forms themselves and the material into which they have been carved. S R

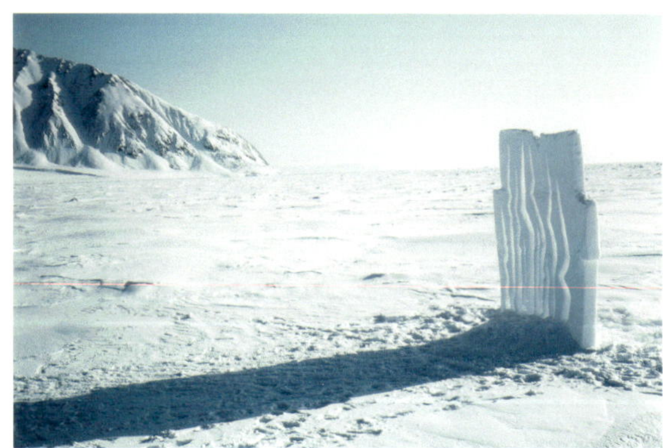

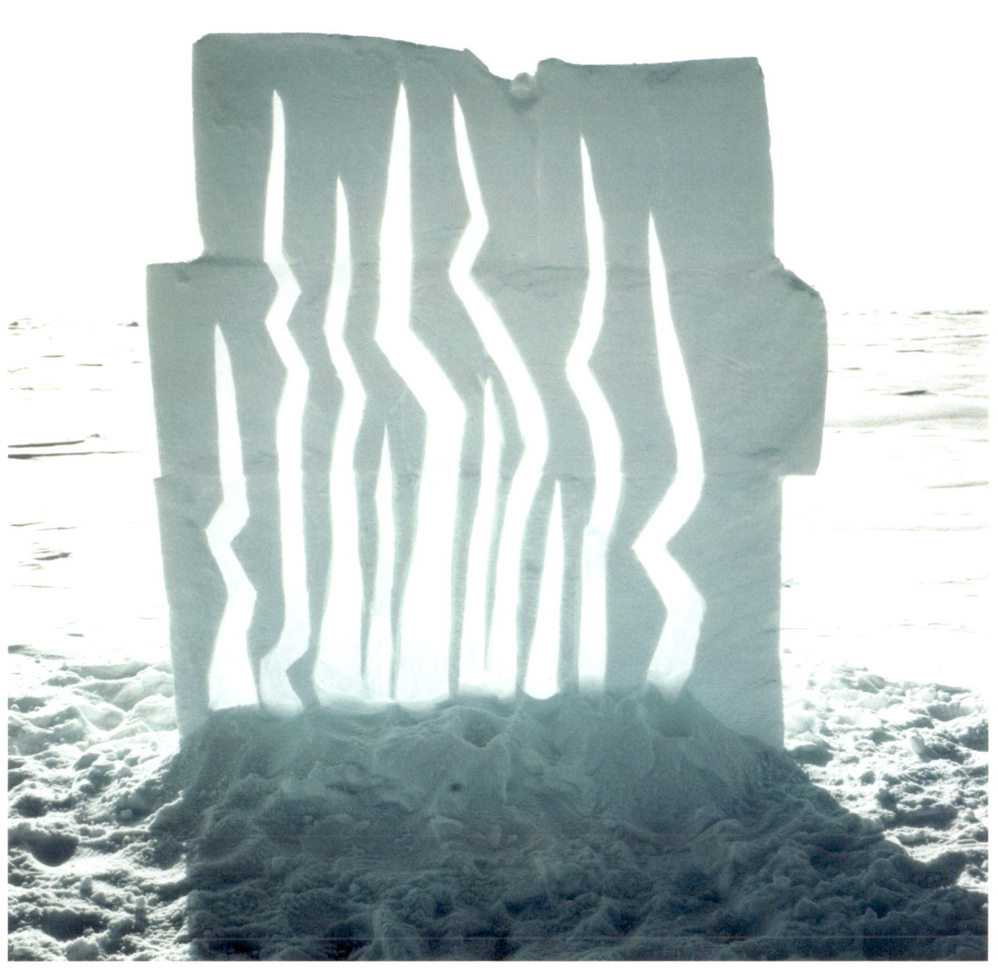

Snow wall, carved into…, Grise Fjord, Ellesmere Island,
2 April 1989, 1989
c-print on cardboard
43 ¼ x 43 x 1 ¾ inches
text work: 14 x 16 inches
Collection of Renée and Paul Mansheim

Hoss Haley creates bold abstract sculptures using industrial materials and fabrication methods. Forcing thick sheets of Cor-Ten steel through an hydraulic press, Haley bends it into elliptical forms which he then composes and assembles. According to Haley, "Because the toric form curves in two directions at once, I am free to assemble structures that are infinitely variable . . . it allows me to create work that is at once simple and complex." *Toric Arch* is as mathematically precise as it is conceptually appealing. Because of its scale, it can be experienced in a manner beyond the visual as viewers can walk though and around it.

Haley's use of simplified forms and gestures aligns him with the tradition of Minimalist sculptors. However, he derives his sources of inspiration from nature and natural processes. His childhood spent in the Great Plains left an indelible mark. The vast landscape is punctuated with solid dwellings that shelter from wind, rain and snow. Monumental grain storage elevators—circular towers that can withstand the force of tons of wheat—are structurally a study in the unification of form and function. *Toric Arch* also references cloud formations: the massive, churning thunderheads that roll over the Plains states are at once billowy and light, yet infused with awe-evoking energy and power. C M H

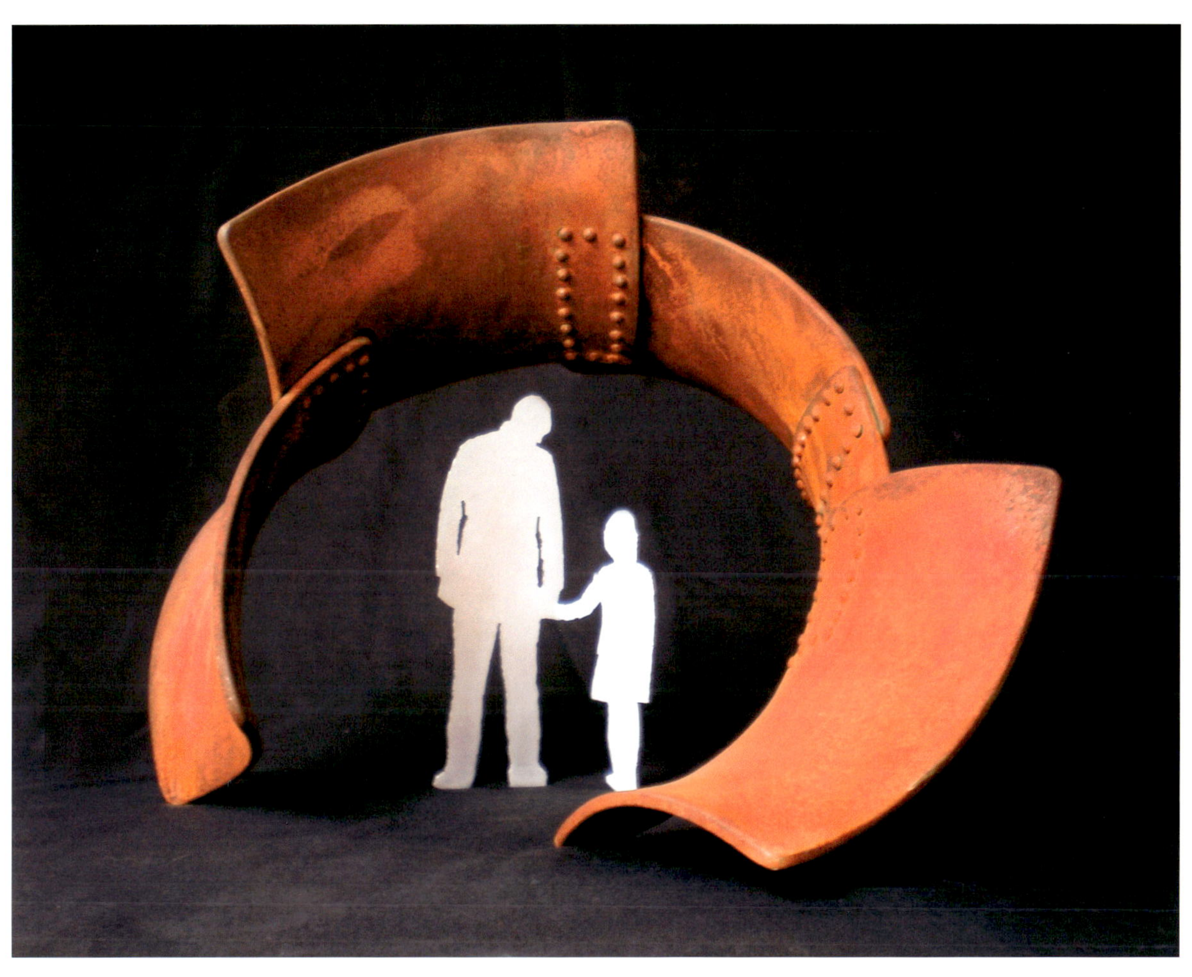

Toric Arch, 2007
Cor-Ten steel
10 ½ x 10 ½ x 13 ½ feet
Collection of Lori and Liam McGee
Courtesy Jole Lassiter Gallery

David **HILLIARD** American, born 1964

David Hilliard has become a master at making the viewers of his photography see exactly what he wants them to see and how he wants them to see it. By photographing the same scene from multiple angles and then seamlessly combining them together, he is able to guide the viewer's eye to interpret the scene exactly as he thinks it should be seen. Usually consisting of two or three panels, Hilliard's photographs are both autobiographical and fictional, dealing with specific circumstances in his life and how they relate to the general experience of living. In *Green*, Hilliard highlights a young boy as he is filling up a watering can. The enlargement of the half-open door makes the scene appear mysterious—even secretive. L B

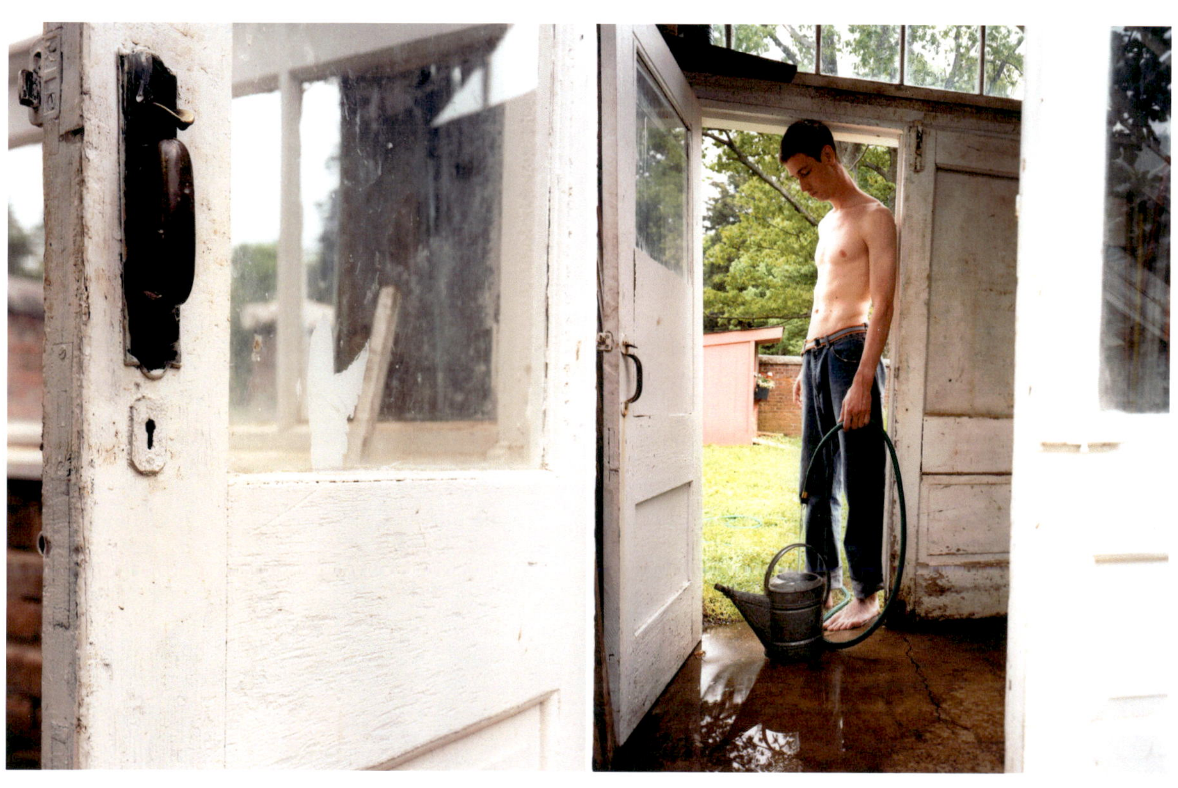

Green (Diptych), 2003
chromogenic print (edition 2/5)
40 x 62 inches
The Frank Konhaus and Ellen Cassilly Collection

Hans HOFMANN German, 1880-1966

One of the most innovative artists to work with abstraction during the first half of the 20th century, Hans Hofmann was inspired by nature and believed that art should always attempt to get closer to what is real. He believed in the spiritual nature of painting, and like Wassily Kandinsky, believed that art (color in particular), expressed emotion. His paintings are best known for what he called their "push and pull"—the way in which their vibrant colors are juxtaposed to create visual tension and resonance. Hofmann's expressive and elegant brushwork also aided in the compositional unity of his paintings.

In the painting *Blue (#9)*, the viewer gets a sense of Hofmann's ideas about "push and pull." The colors contrast starkly with one another; some appearing to move forward, others appearing to recede, creating a distinct sense of depth and space. The influences of Fauvism and Cubism, as well as the artists Kandinsky and Paul Cézanne, can all be seen within this elegant painting. S R

Blue (#9), 1962
oil on paper/canvas
24 x 19 ½ inches
Collection of Thomas E. Kanes and Susan Valentine Kanes

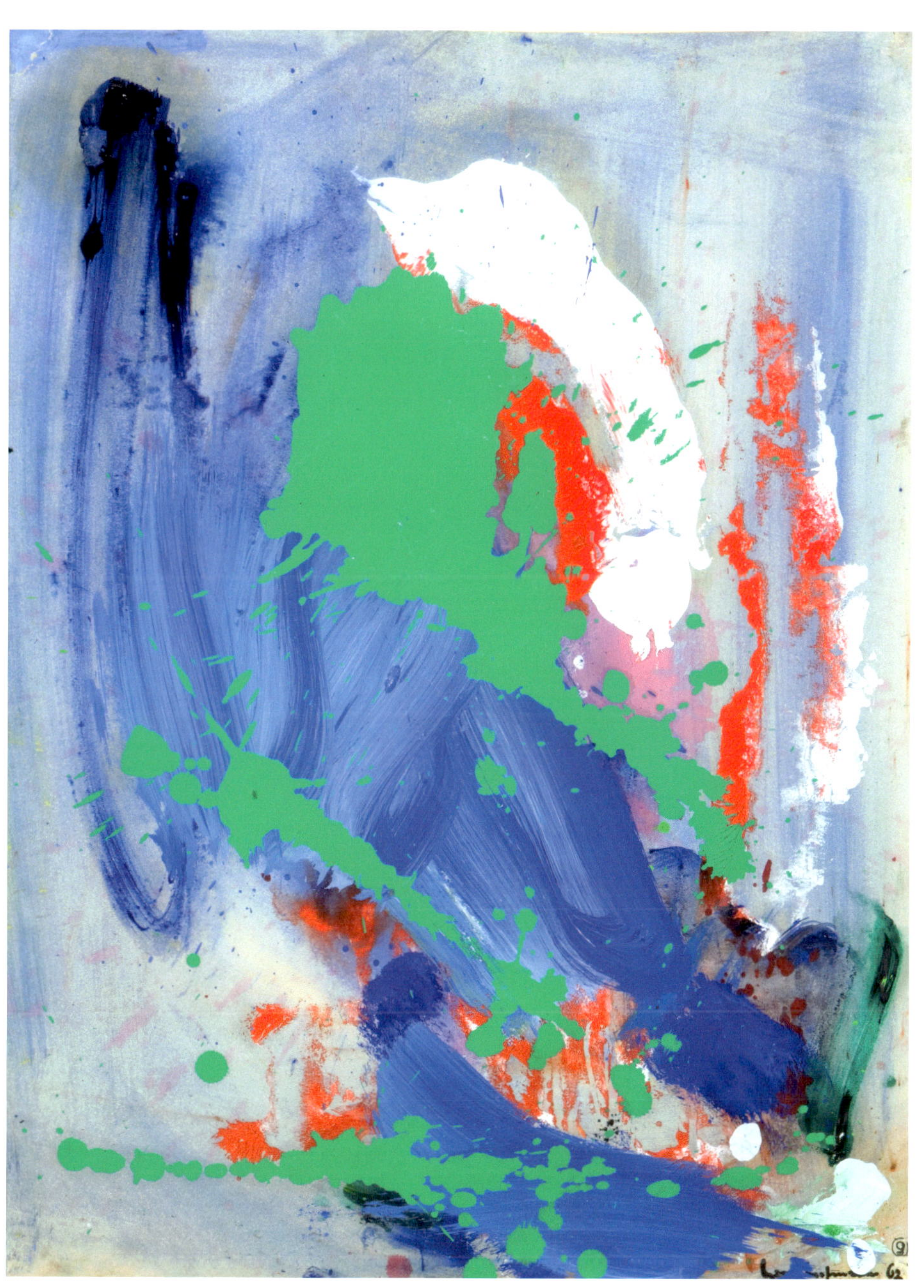

Herb Jackson's drawing *P 82* is built layer upon layer, an additive process that results in a resonant balance between surface modulation and the illusion of depth. Jackson's choice of colors and materials lends the drawing a radiant quality, as the intense yellow hues interact with somber cobalt blues. In the same way that many of Jackson's paintings are constructed of layers of scraped paint, the forms and marks in this drawing are created by applications of layers of pigment so that the underlying colors show through, as well as delicately incised lines that contribute to its compelling surface texture. The combination of these qualities reveals the importance of the interplay between process and chance that is so essential to Jackson's work. Through both masking and revealing, Jackson lends intrigue and even mystery to his work. Embracing multiple perspectives, Jackson states that "my inner journey through art confirms for me, at least, that it is not necessary to rob life of its mystery in order to understand it." CMH

P 82, 1981
oil crayon and pencil on paper
30 x 22 inches
Collection of Ann D. Frisch

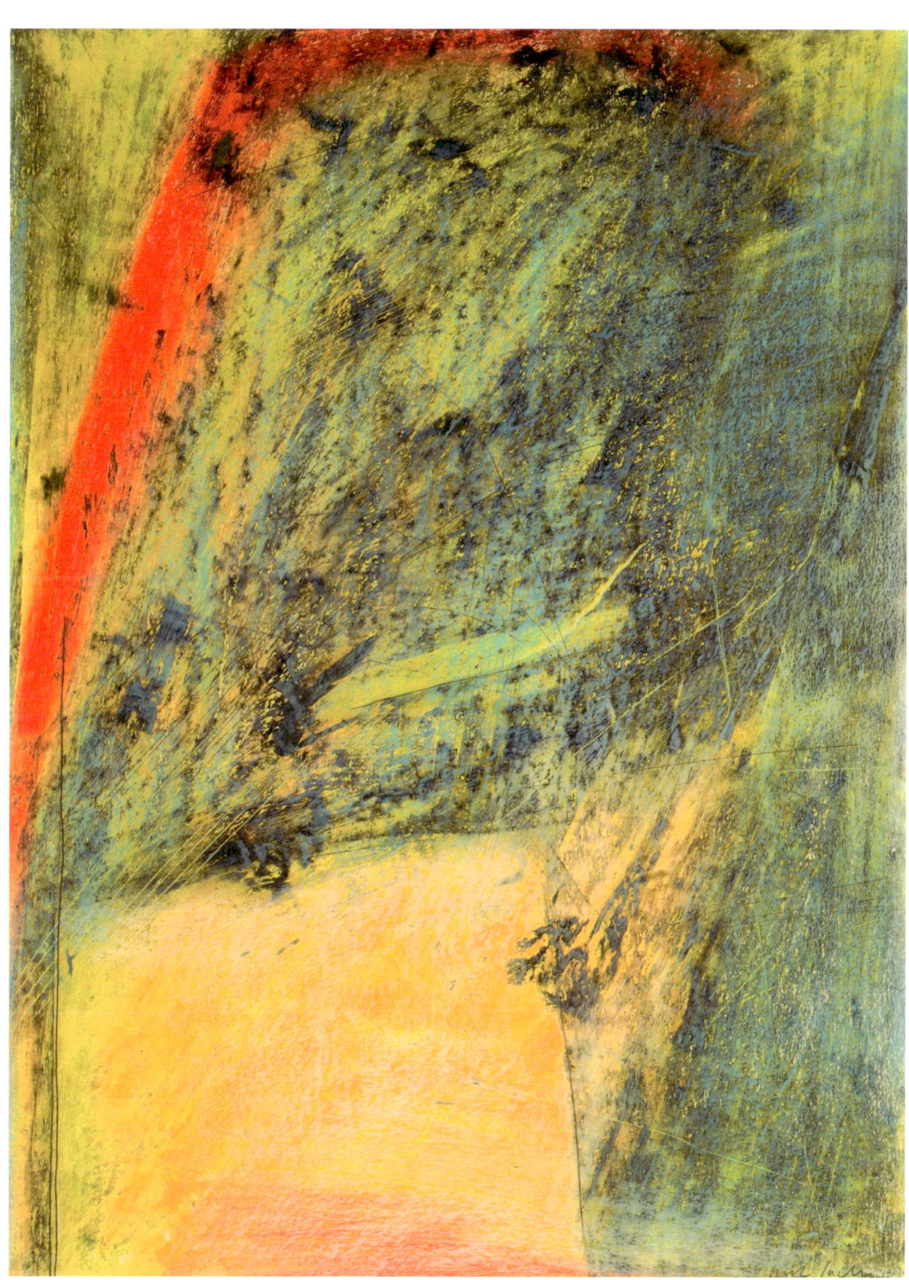

Josef KOUDELKA   Czech, born 1938

Josef Koudelka gained fame by photographing his impoverished countrymen in the former Czechoslovakia. His dark, foreboding photographs capture the injustices enacted upon these people but also reveal the strength and dignity of the human spirit—a common theme throughout his work.

Koudelka chooses to live a simple, transient existence, literally living out of a sleeping bag. Taking as many pictures as he can, Koudelka often returns to the same spot year after year to capture the scene over time and see if he can improve upon his past efforts. His general approach to photography is to take it to the "maximum," striving tirelessly to get the best composition, the best subject, the best photograph. Despite the documentary quality of his work, he does not consider himself a photojournalist.

This untitled photograph is an example of Koudelka's more recent work, which features landscapes devoid of humans, yet filled with markers of human presence. Trash and debris are scattered in the foreground, and the expansive distant landscape (a massive strip mine) shows the indelible scar left by humans who mined coal from this area for centuries. S R

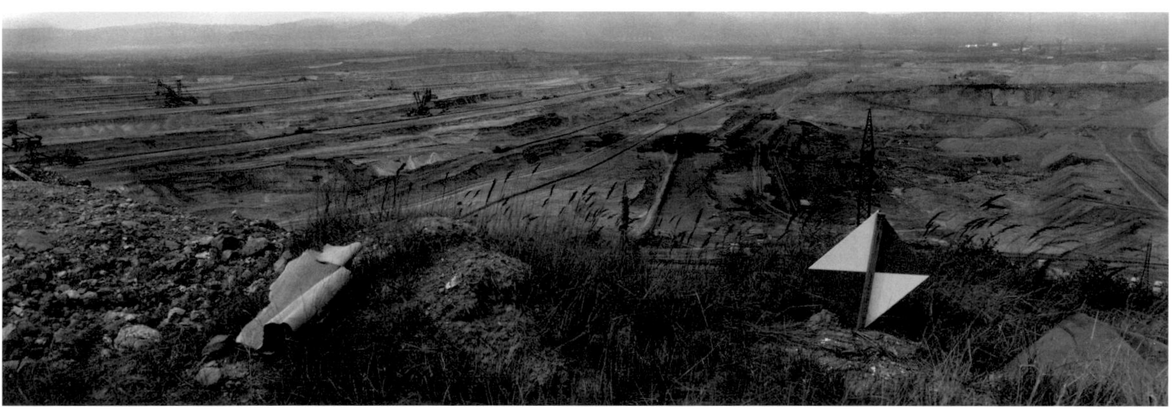

Untitled (Coal mining Started in the Region around the year 1400), 1991
gelatin silver print
14 x 41 inches
Anonymous lender

Jonathan LASKER American, born 1948

Jonathan Lasker's paintings are a blend of automatic (or stream-of-consciousness) forms and carefully orchestrated examinations of art historical works. Painstakingly composing through numerous sketches, he reinterprets works from Classicism to Mannerism to Expressionism in a bold, abstract manner. Lasker uses different techniques to apply paint to the various elements of his compositions, which create the illusion of spatial depth. The resulting paintings are abstract and yet vaguely figurative, emphasizing relationships between foreground and background and highlighting the various connections between disparate elements within the painting.

The Oddness Factor's receding, cross-hatched background is strikingly different from the mass of blue, yellow and mauve lines in the foreground. The vertically lined form in the center of the composition emerges from the background and is linked to the colorful brushstrokes by a red circular form. These relationships appear to set up some sort of enigmatic narrative, but the story is trapped somewhere between memory and dream or consciousness and the subconscious, not yet manifesting itself in recognizable imagery. S R

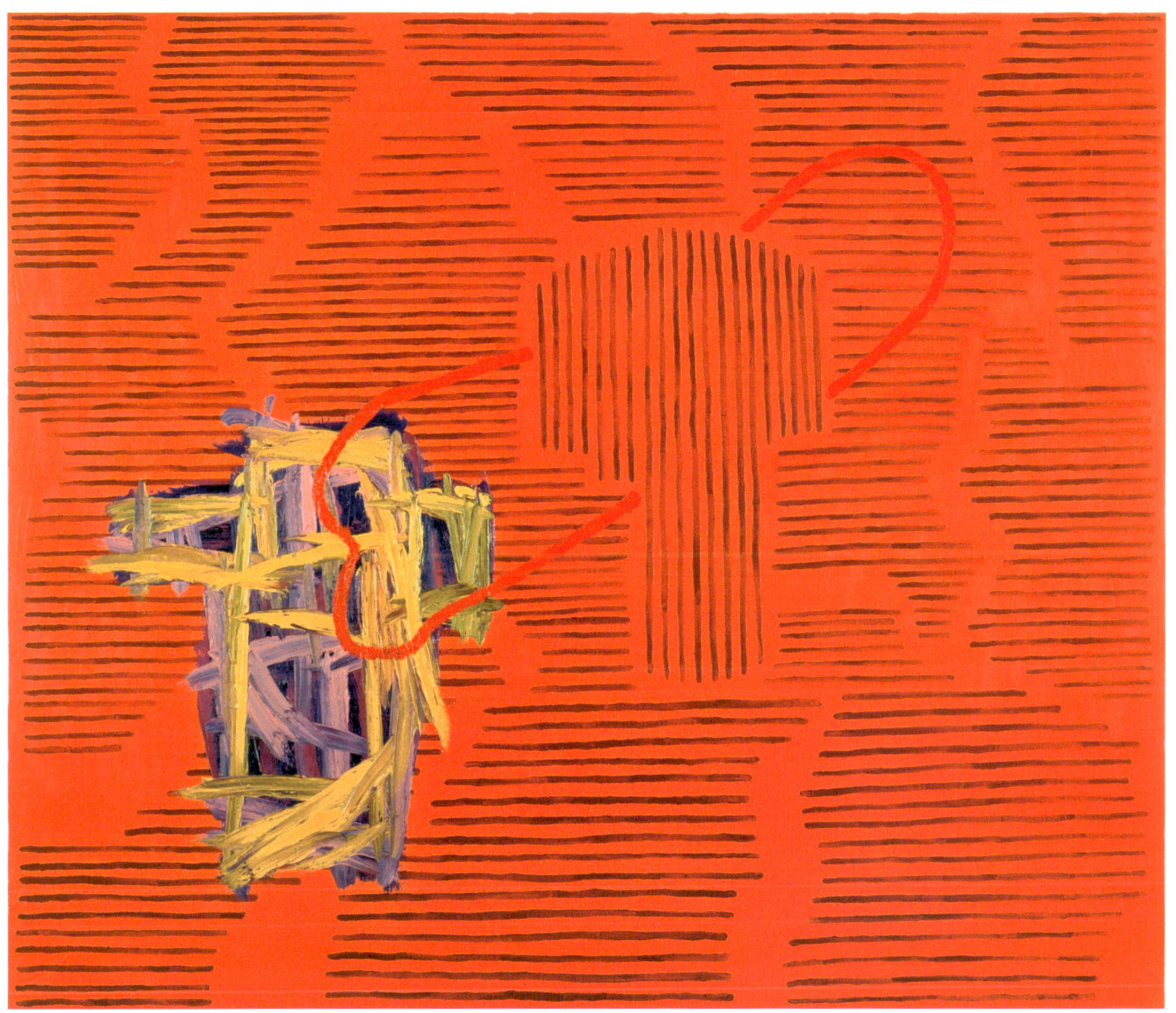

The Oddness Factor, 1985
oil on linen
59 x 71 inches
Collection of Jean Crutchfield and Robert Hobbs
Courtesy of the Artist and Cheim & Read, New York

Charles LeDRAY American, born 1960

Charles LeDray chooses to situate his work in the enigmatic terrain somewhere between art, fashion and craft. Drawing upon a variety of materials, including human bone, he commonly works in miniature. LeDray pays careful attention to the smallest details in all of his pieces, which adds to their whimsical folk quality. As elusive as the classification of the work is its ultimate meaning. LeDray offers no explanation, and states that his personal motivation in creating these evocative objects is the desire to change a material into something else. But beyond their comfortable and homey appearance, these objects strike the viewer with the suggestion that they have a specific story to tell and a life behind them. *Untitled/Hoop* is no different, as the unoccupied sleeves of brightly colored miniature shirts and dresses are linked into a circle. The viewer is left with the feeling that the very garments themselves are alive, making a circle like children on a playground. L B

Untitled/Hoop, 1994
fabric, thread, embroidery floss, metal, beads, buttons, wood, wire
5 ½ x 49 ½ x 2 ½ inches
Collection of Randy Shull and Hedy Fischer
Courtesy of Sperone Westwater, New York

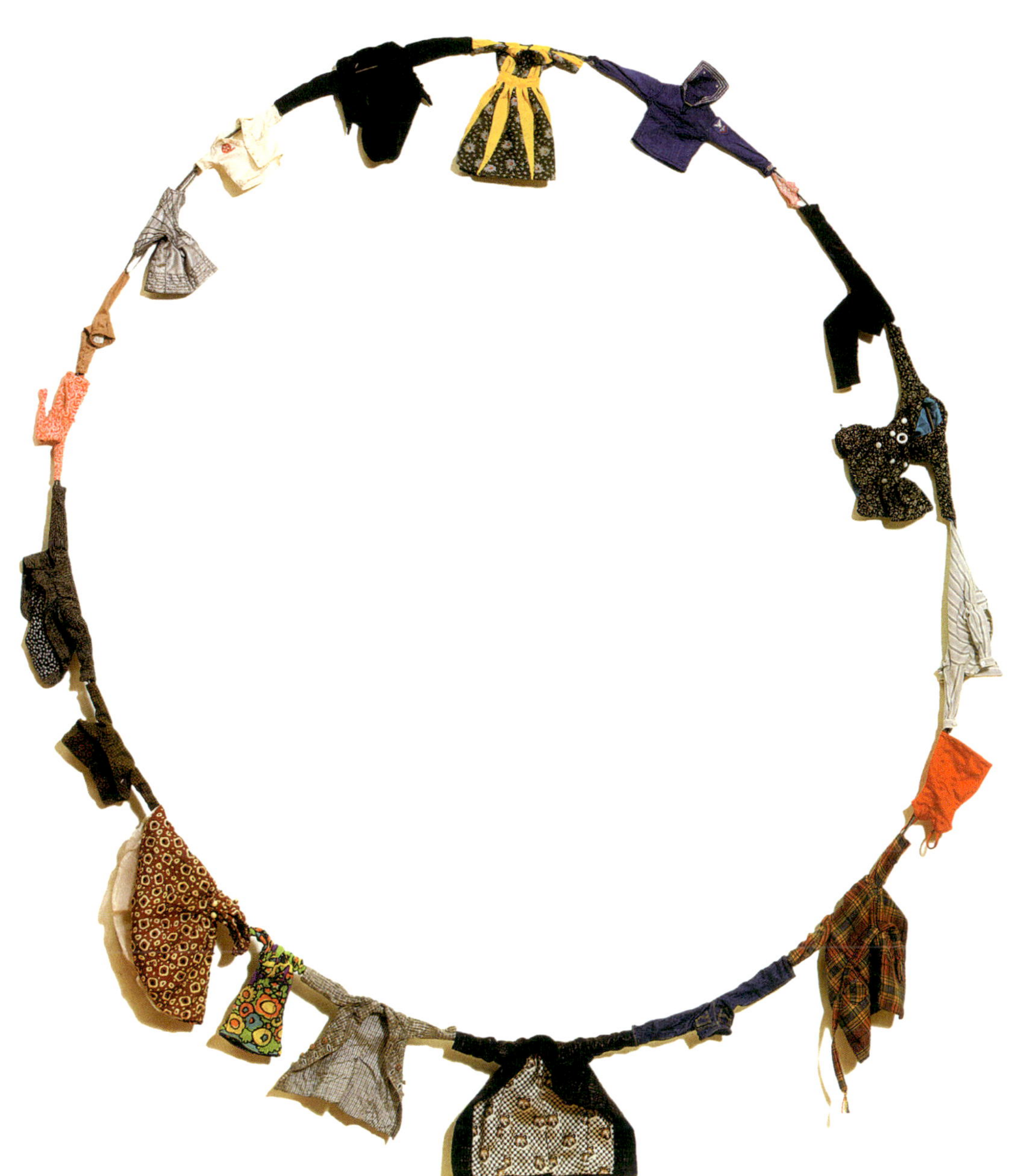

Hung Liu left Maoist regime China to settle in Northern California, where she has become known for her images that juxtapose haunting figures with gracefully serene settings. Drawing from photographs of recent Chinese social history, she interlays her scenes with symbols from the culture's classical visual history, notably flowers and birds. Liu calls the result "witnesses from China's past, overlooking and commenting upon events from its modern era." In *Towards Peng-Lai (Paradise)*, Liu references a photograph of unclothed, gaunt oarsmen. The laborers' oars intertwine with plum blossoms, a traditional symbol of resilience against adversity, and support a stylized Chinese bird. In Chinese mythology, Penglai Mountain is the paradise home of the Eight Immortals. In so titling and reworking the original photograph, Liu turns the harsh lives of these figures into a hopeful journey towards paradise. E B

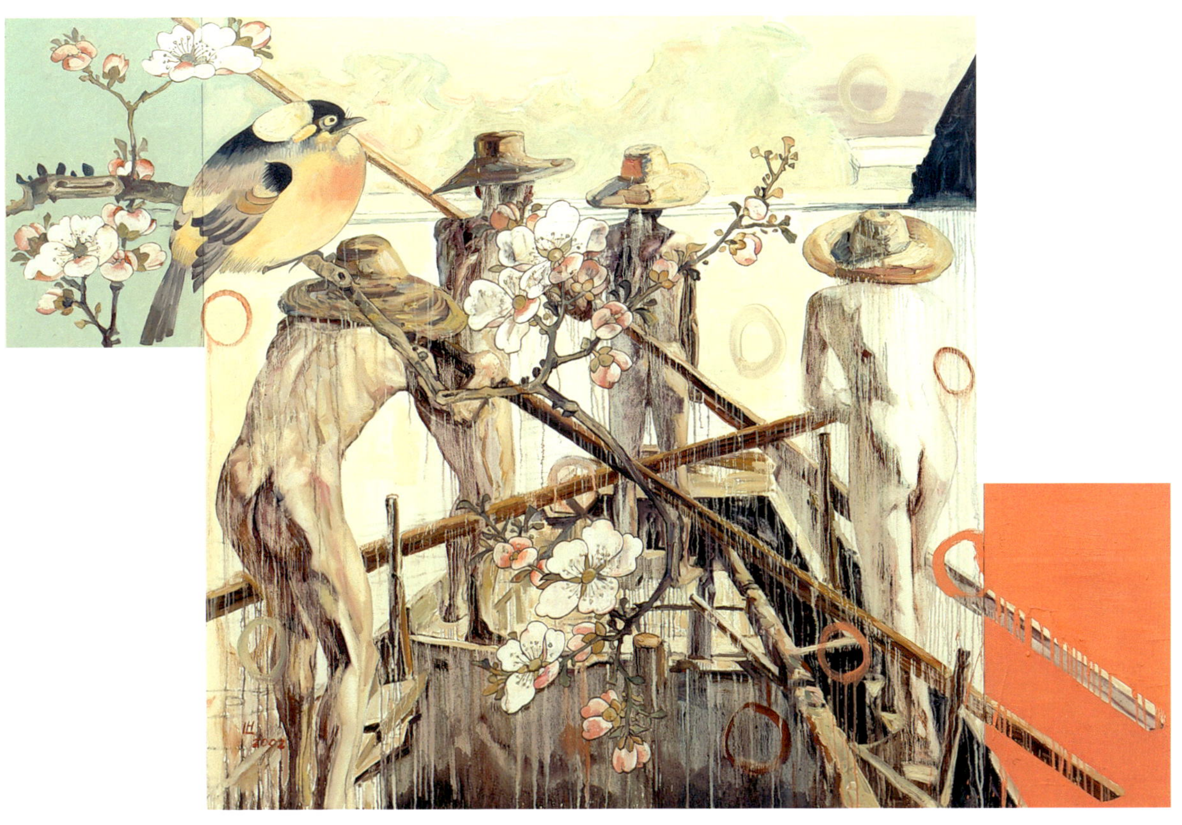

Towards Peng-Lai (Paradise), 2002
oil on canvas
72 x 108 inches
Collection of Randy Shull and Hedy Fischer
Courtesy of Rena Bransten Gallery, San Francisco, California

Loretta LUX German, born 1969

Although photography is the German-born artist Loretta Lux's primary medium, she manages to draw upon her background in painting as well, fusing these two traditionally disparate realms. In Lux's striking, digitally-enhanced photographs, children stare out at the viewer, framed by sparse, hand-painted backdrops. Working for months on one image, Lux builds her compositions from scratch as a painter does. She meticulously dresses and arranges her sitters, later dropping their photographs into backgrounds from her own travels or paintings, and then delicately adjusting the children's features using Photoshop. The result is a hybrid between luminous Renaissance paintings, especially those of Bronzino and Diego Velázquez, and wide-eyed Japanese anime style. What Lux calls her "imaginary portraits" are more about the idealization of childhood than straightforward portraits of the children depicted. In both *Girl with Crossed Arms* and *Isabella*, Lux's pastel palette heightens the captivatingly eerie quality that has earned her oeuvre descriptions ranging from charming to monstrous. E B

__Girl with Crossed Arms__, 2001
Ilfochrome
11 ¾ x 11 ¾ inches
Collection of Lucinda W. Bunnen
Courtesy of the Artist and Yossi Milo Gallery

__Isabella__, 2001
Ilfochrome
11 ¾ x 11 ¾ inches
Collection of Allen Thomas Jr., Wilson, North Carolina
Courtesy of the Artist and Yossi Milo Gallery

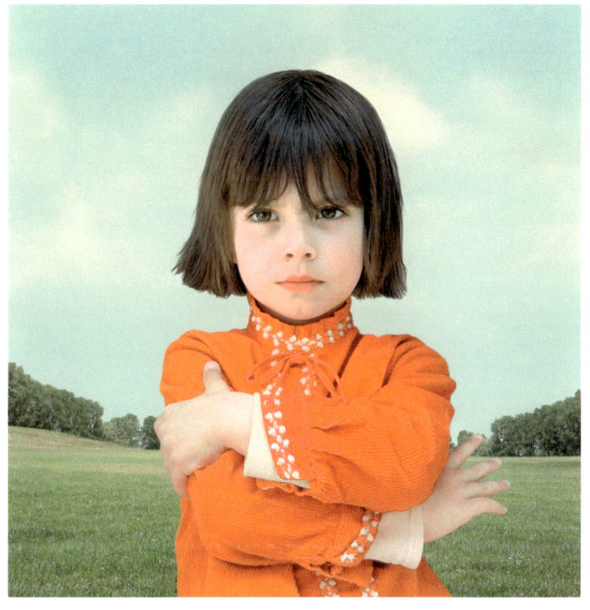

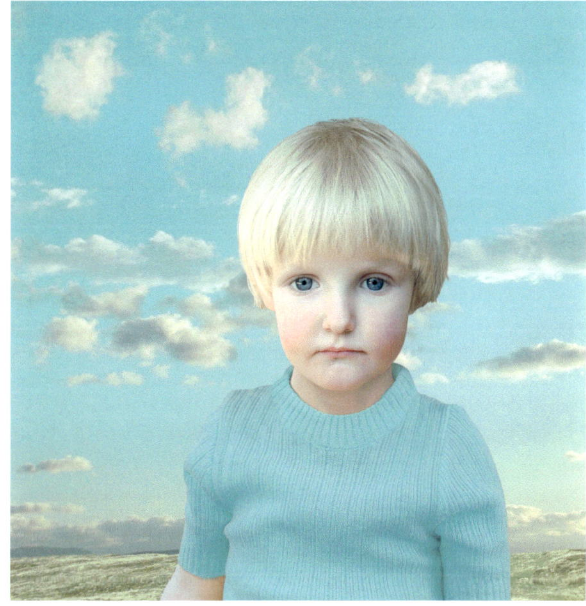

83

Sally MANN American, born 1951

Living and working in her hometown of Lexington, Virginia, Sally Mann masterfully portrays the personal, from intimate portraits of her children to haunting evocations of the Southern landscape. Mann came into prominence for the photographs she created in collaboration with her three children, at times staged and at others shot in moments of serendipity. "We are spinning a story of what it is to grow up," reflects Mann. "It is a complicated story and sometimes we try to take on the grand themes: anger, love, death, sensuality and beauty." *Jessie Bites* and *Virginia at Nine* convey some of the daily struggles and complicated emotions experienced in childhood, as well as a magical sensuality. These portraits attest that Mann has entered the primal world of childhood, capturing it from a child's rather than an adult's perspective.

Mann's more recent landscapes of the rural South conjure a rich, romantic essence of place and history. These large gelatin silver prints are manipulated—toned with tea, shot through antique lenses and printed from negatives which revive complex 19th century techniques including the wet-collodian process. Mann alludes to timelessness in these evocative "portraits" that both celebrate and eulogize a particular place. C M H

Untitled (Deep South #5), 1998
gelatin silver enlargement print, toned with tea (edition 3/10)
47 x 37 ¼ inches
Collection of Allen Thomas, Jr., Wilson, North Carolina

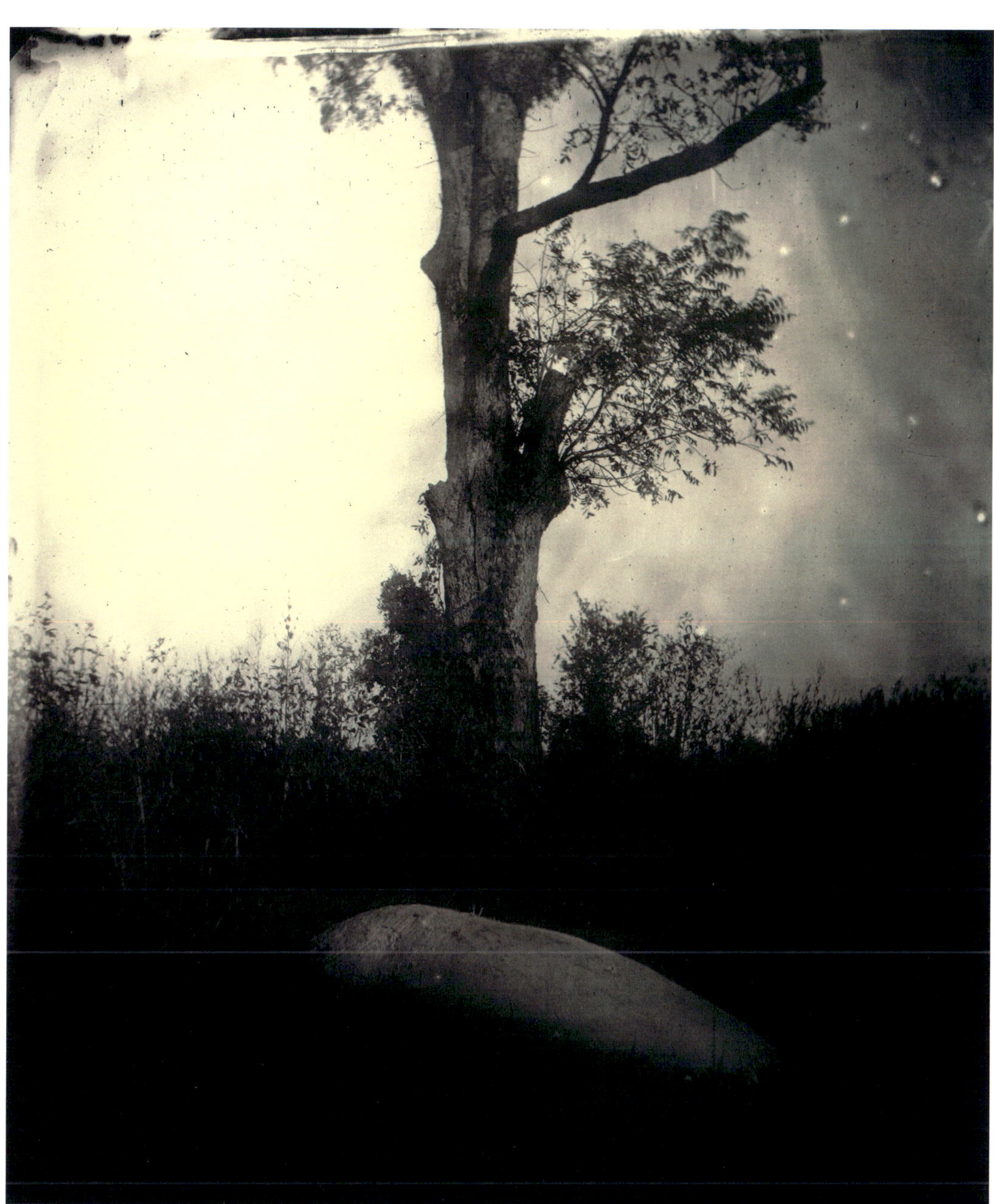

Jessie Bites, 1985
gelatin silver print (edition 20/25)
20 x 24 inches
Anonymous lender

Virginia at Nine, 1994/2000
toned gelatin silver print (edition 17/25)
8 x 10 inches
The Frank Konhaus and Ellen Cassilly Collection

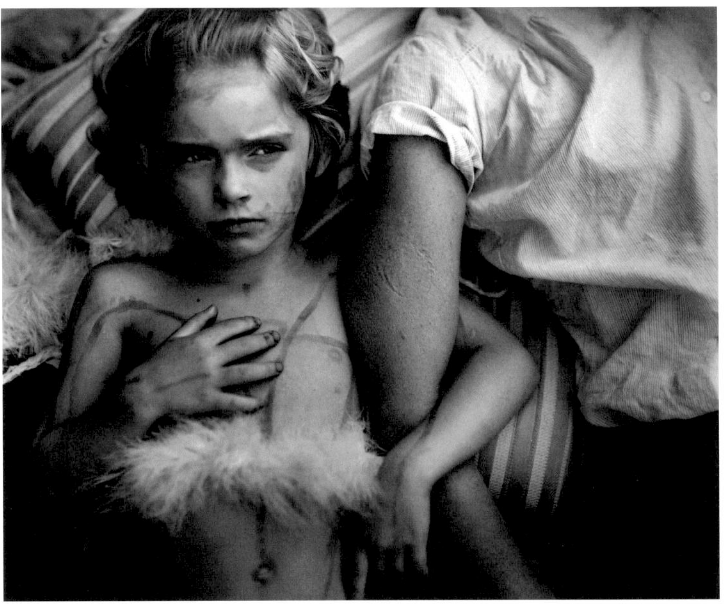

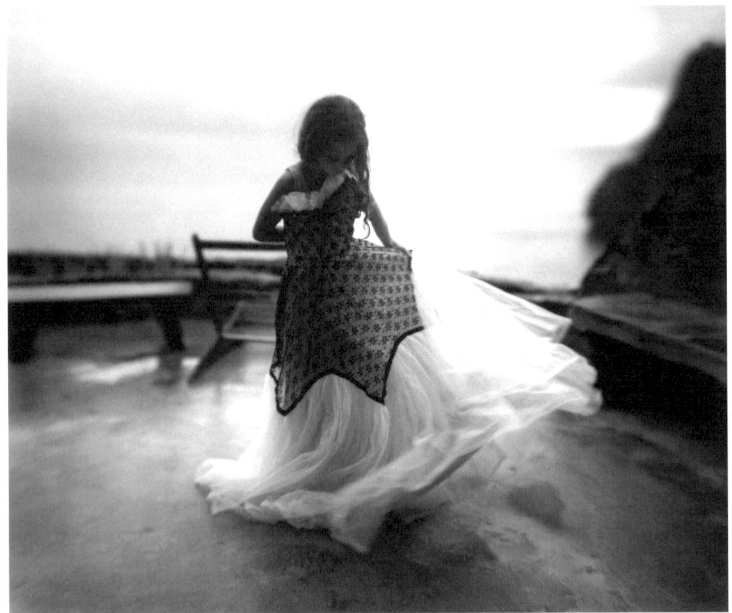

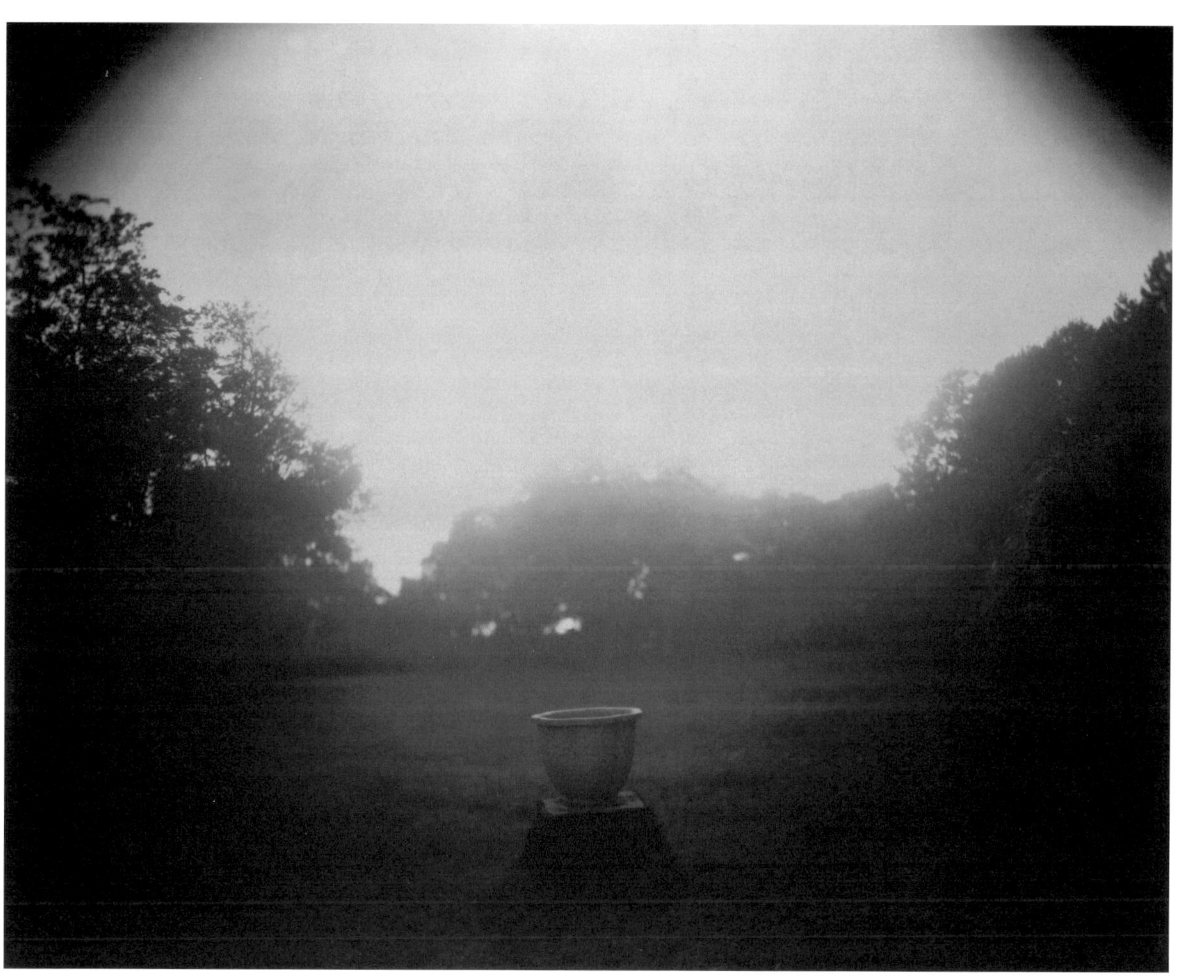

Untitled, from the Mother Land: Virginia Series, 1992
gelatin silver enlargement print, toned with tea
32 ½ x 40 ½ inches
Collection of Allen Thomas, Jr., Wilson, North Carolina

Painter Tom McGrath has gained notoriety as a landscape artist. His depictions are more concerned with capturing the viewer's movement through the landscape than with portraying it accurately. Inspired by the experience of driving in a car through the American terrain, McGrath aims to explore the optical distortions of the landscape as viewed from the perspective of a speeding car. He uses oil paint not only as a medium, but also as a tool for accomplishing his goals, sculpting and shaping it on the canvas into a variety of textures to help the viewer visualize the intersection of time and space that McGrath perceives so clearly. In *Untitled (pastoral landscape)*, the entire image seems to be compressed and the wind has become a tangible, visible force, arching and swirling across the canvas, trapping the light and dwarfing the lone tree, distorting the viewer's understanding of their relationship to the unfolding scene. L B

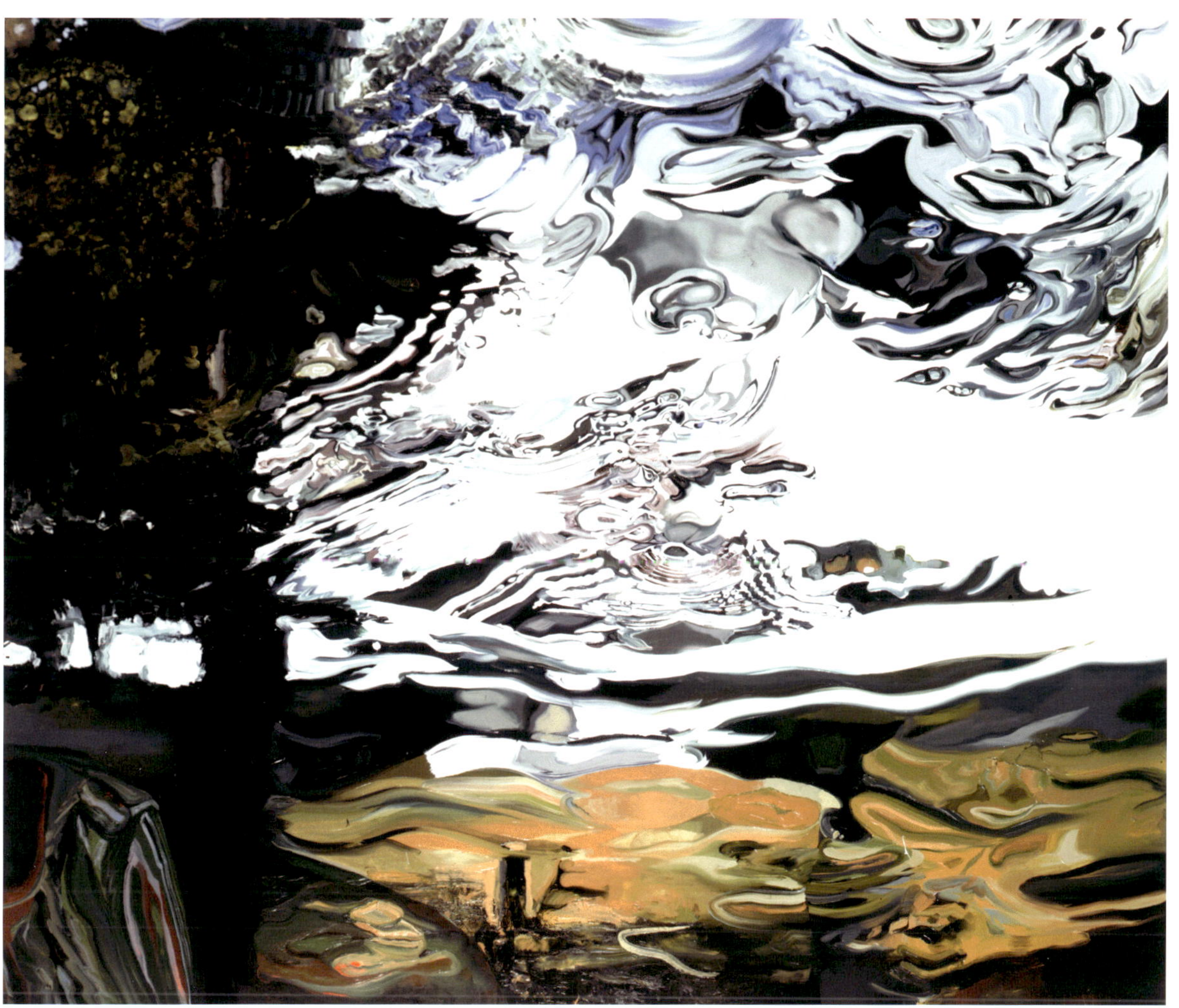

Untitled (pastoral landscape), 2004
oil on canvas
60 x 72 inches
Collection of Paul and Sara Monroe

Jason **MEADOWS**   American, born 1972

The provocative visual presence of Jason Meadows' *Monster* reveals
his aptitude for combining geometric formalism with do-it-yourself
craftsmanship. Utilizing industrially crafted brackets and bolts to assemble
intensely colored forms into a concise and cohesive sculpture, Meadows'
work exhibits the ethos of Modernism—its celebration of democratic,
mass-produced materials. His work departs from the supposed purity
of Modernist abstraction, however, into an altogether more subjective,
ambiguous, even ironic realm. Meadows' treatment of slick, mass-produced
materials is tempered with a respect for the poetic qualities that these
substances invariably retain.

Sited directly on the floor, this sculpture approximates human scale so that
one's interaction with it is immediate and direct, not mediated by a pedestal
or plinth. While this particular work exudes control and precision, the raw
wood that intersects the synthetic blue forms pits surface and sincerity
against one another as though to discover which will hold sway. C M H

Monster, 2000
MDF, wood, paint, aluminum and metal
48 x 48 x 34 inches
Collection of Paul and Sara Monroe

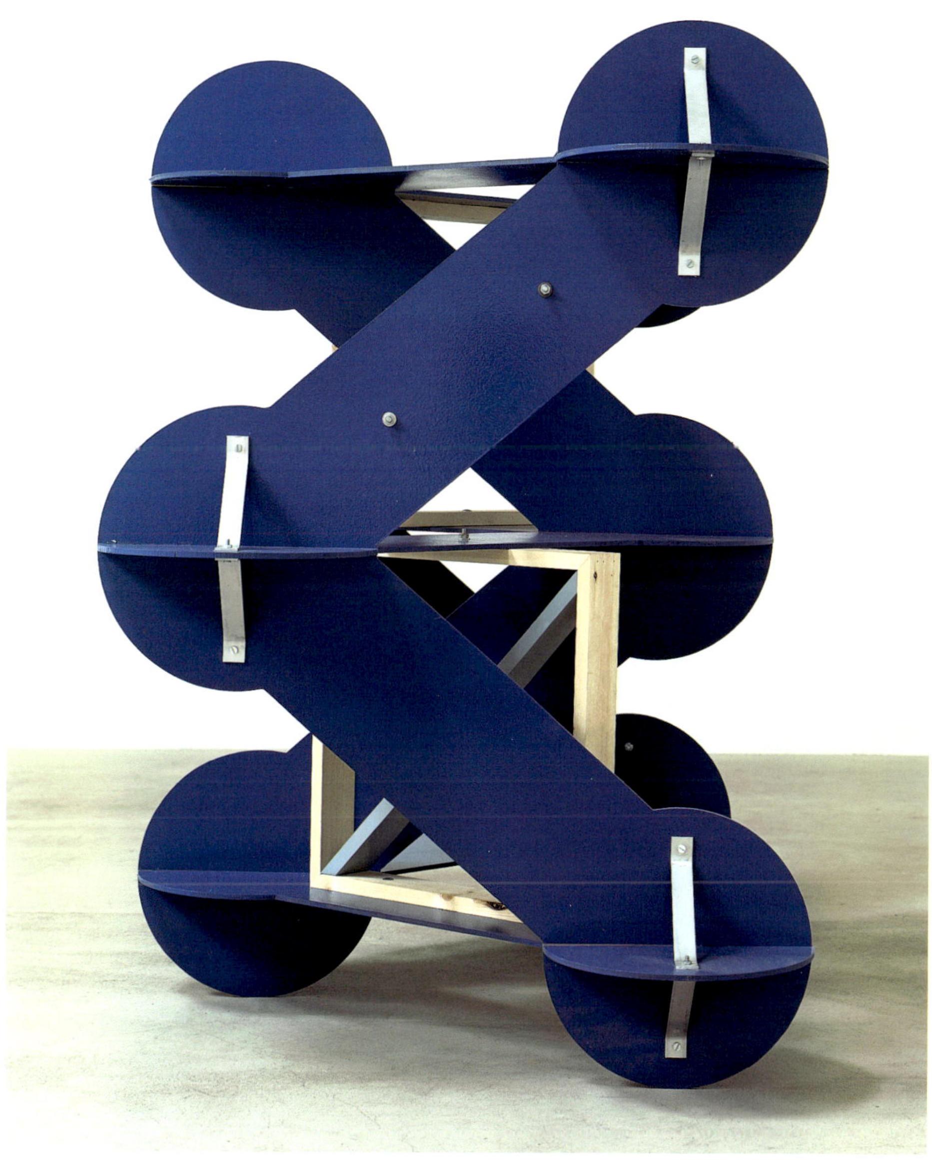

91

Joan MITCHELL American, 1925-1992

Joan Mitchell utilized vigorous strokes of color and fluid forms to convey evocations of nature. "My paintings aren't about art issues," she stated. "They're about a feeling that comes to me from the outside, from landscape." Her selection of color referenced the setting: the time of day, season and temperature, while atmosphere, weather and the quality of light are referenced by the nature of the strokes she employed (thick, thin, textured or broken). Mitchell's specific vocabulary developed over time as she devised bold ways to use line and color that enabled her to translate her feelings into signs and to capture her responses to the landscape and the emotions evoked by her settings.

In *Fields II*, Mitchell used color sparingly, composing with only blue, black and the whiteness of the paper untouched by ink. This reserved print exudes a coolness and dormancy, suggesting that the fields are fallow, or that the black earth has been plowed in preparation for winter. Notably, *Fields II* was the final print that Mitchell created before her death in 1992. C M H

Fields II, 1992
color aquatint etching (edition 6/13)
23 x 16 ½ inches
Collection of Thomas E. Kanes and Susan Valentine Kanes

Phil MOODY British, born 1949

Utilizing overlapping layers of rich and evocative imagery and text, Phil Moody explores the history and culture of the textile industry in South Carolina. The text is usually taken from interviews and conversations that Moody has with the mill workers. He challenges the viewer to think about these workers, an especially poignant and timely meditation because of the plight of those who have lost their jobs with the recent closings of numerous mills. *Angelus* offers an oblique reference to an 1857 painting, *The Angelus*, by Jean-Francois Millet, which depicts farmers taking a break from their toils in the field to recite the Angelus prayer, a devotional performed as a church bell is rung in honor of the Incarnation. S R

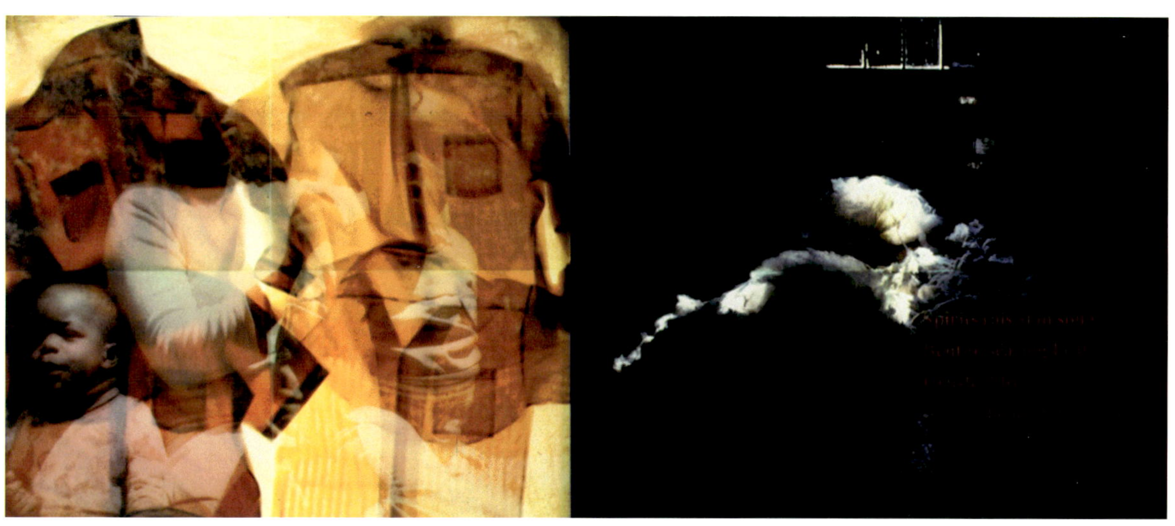

Angelus, 1998
Ilfochrome photo diptych
32 x 80 inches
Goodrich Corporation Collection
Courtesy of Joie Lassiter Gallery

Andrew MOORE American, born 1957

Andrew Moore's complex portrait within a portrait, shot within a home in Havana, conveys an intense reliquary-like quality. The primary subject is a glamorous pre-Castro photograph of Margarita Heymann y Boza. Visible through a mottled mirror behind this portrait is a sumptuous interior reflecting ethereal light and color. Golden chairs and frames and an etched crystal bottle are peripheral elements that Moore uses to impart the beauty of the environs. The individuals portrayed within this composition seem frozen in time: both the debutante photograph of Margarita and the paintings of her grandparents situated in the room's corner. Moore's photograph is as elegant as it is technically precise. His elegiac portrayal of interior details reveals something of the fluidity of history and the indeterminacy of a place that is marking time. C M H

96

Margarita, Havana Cuba, 1999
c-print (edition 3/5)
50 x 40 inches
The Frank Konhaus and Ellen Cassilly Collection

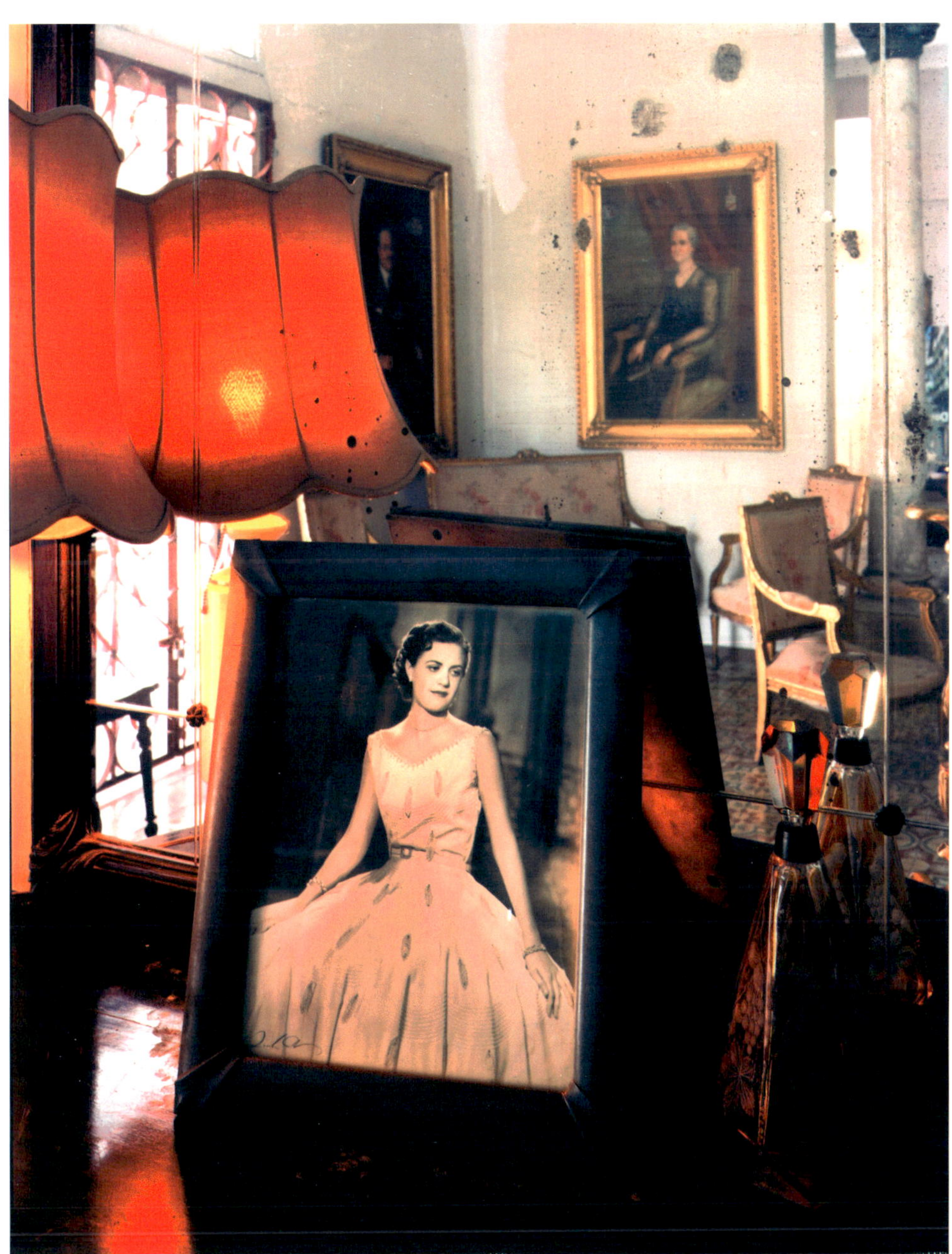

Robert MOTHERWELL American, 1915-1991

Robert Motherwell was one of the youngest artists in the group known as the New York School in the mid-20th century and served as the rational voice of Abstract Expressionism through his essays and lectures. Unlike his more temperamental peers Jackson Pollock and Willem de Kooning, Motherwell discussed art as "a series of oral decisions about the aesthetic." He viewed abstraction philosophically as the elimination of all but the most necessary, while also acknowledging a debt to Surrealism and other past movements. Noted for his bold brushwork and use of striking contrasts of black paint on canvas, Motherwell experimented with a wide range of media, including painting, printmaking and collage. To Motherwell, collage represented "the 20th century's greatest innovation" and served as modern still life—his often included copies of objects from his own life, like wine or cheese labels. *Untitled (Blue with Brown on Beige)* represents this autobiographical tendency and Motherwell's shift in his later work away from the intense simplification of his earlier years. E B

Untitled (Blue with Brown on Beige), 1990
acrylic, pencil, oil and paper collage on canvas board
20 x 16 inches
Collection of Jancy and Gilbert Patrick, North Carolina
Courtesy of Jerald Melberg Gallery

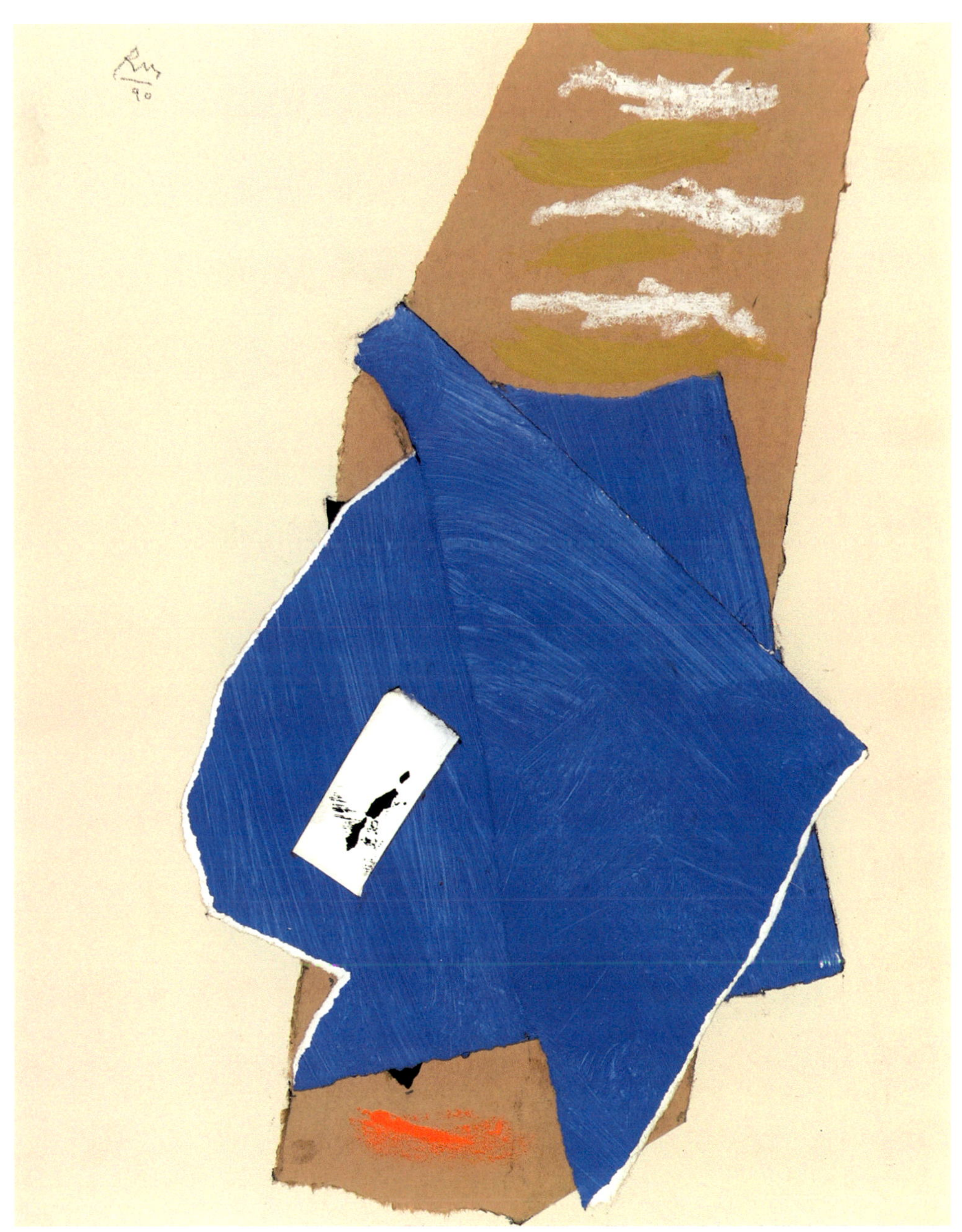

Vik MUNIZ Brazilian, born 1961

This work is from the avant-garde Brazilian artist Vik Muniz's series titled *Pictures of Junk.* In his earlier work, Muniz created and photographed images made of peanut butter and jelly, toy soldiers, cotton and dust. For this series, Muniz literally uses scraps of garbage to recreate history paintings by well-known artists. This particular work shows Orestes being assaulted by the Furies, who are inflicting their anger upon him for murdering his mother. The Furies, also known as the Erinyes (The Angry Ones), were known to ceaselessly torment the unlucky souls who had not atoned for their sins. When Orestes was taken to trial by the Olympian gods and found not guilty, the unsatisfied Furies continued their taunting until Orestes sacrificed a sheep in their name. To create this image and the others in the series, Muniz stood on a scaffold above a team of students and outlined the figures with a laser pointer. Once the composition was complete, Muniz created his photograph from this bird's-eye vantage point. L B

Pictures of Junk: Orestes pursued by the Furies, after William-Adolphe Bouguereau, 2006
digital c-print (a.p. 2/4)
50 x 40 inches
Private Collection, Dr. W. Kent Davis, Raleigh, North Carolina
Courtesy of Rena Bransten Gallery, San Francisco, California

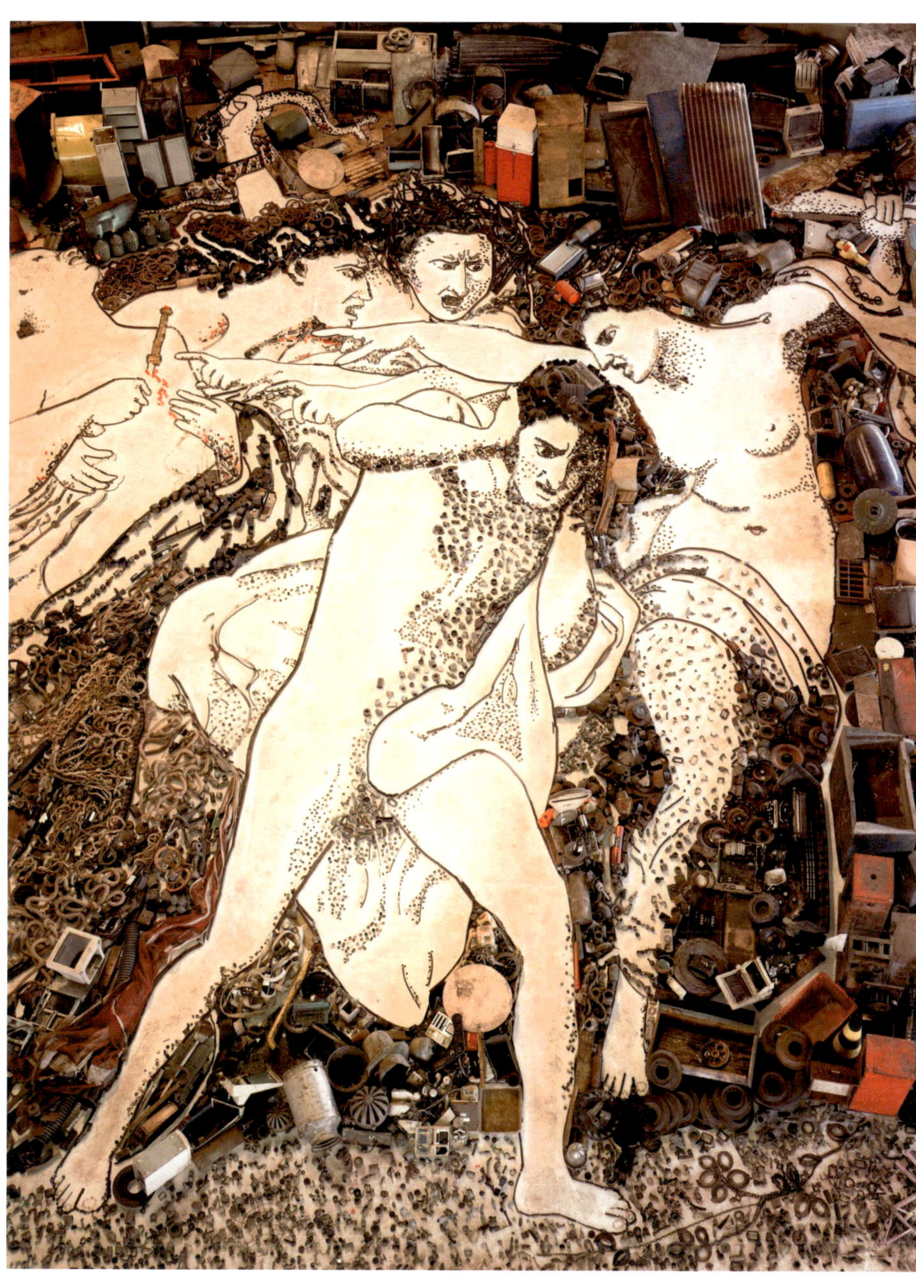

Elizabeth MURRAY American, 1940-2007

Elizabeth Murray's brightly colored abstract canvases investigate the possibilities of form to create the illusion of three-dimensional space. Often employing shaped canvases that jut out from the wall, Murray playfully challenged the boundary between painting as a sculptural object and painting as a pictorial realm. Her paintings frequently allude to domestic objects or articles of clothing, such as cups, chairs, tables and shoes; however, these still-lifes always remain somewhat abstract.

The monumental painting *Split and Join* illustrates the effectiveness of bold, complementary colors (red and green) to create visual resonance against a hot pink background. Reminiscent of strategies employed by Paul Cézanne and Henri Matisse, Murray implies three-dimensional space by a thin, vertical white line that weaves in and out of the curvy red form on the left. The two flat halves of the heart-like form intersect at one juncture, and a bulbous, purple line connects both sides at the top. These suggestive forms also underscore Murray's fascination with dream states and the psychological challenges of domestic life. C M H

102

Split and Join, 1980
oil on canvas
133 x 132 inches
On Loan from the Bank of America Collection

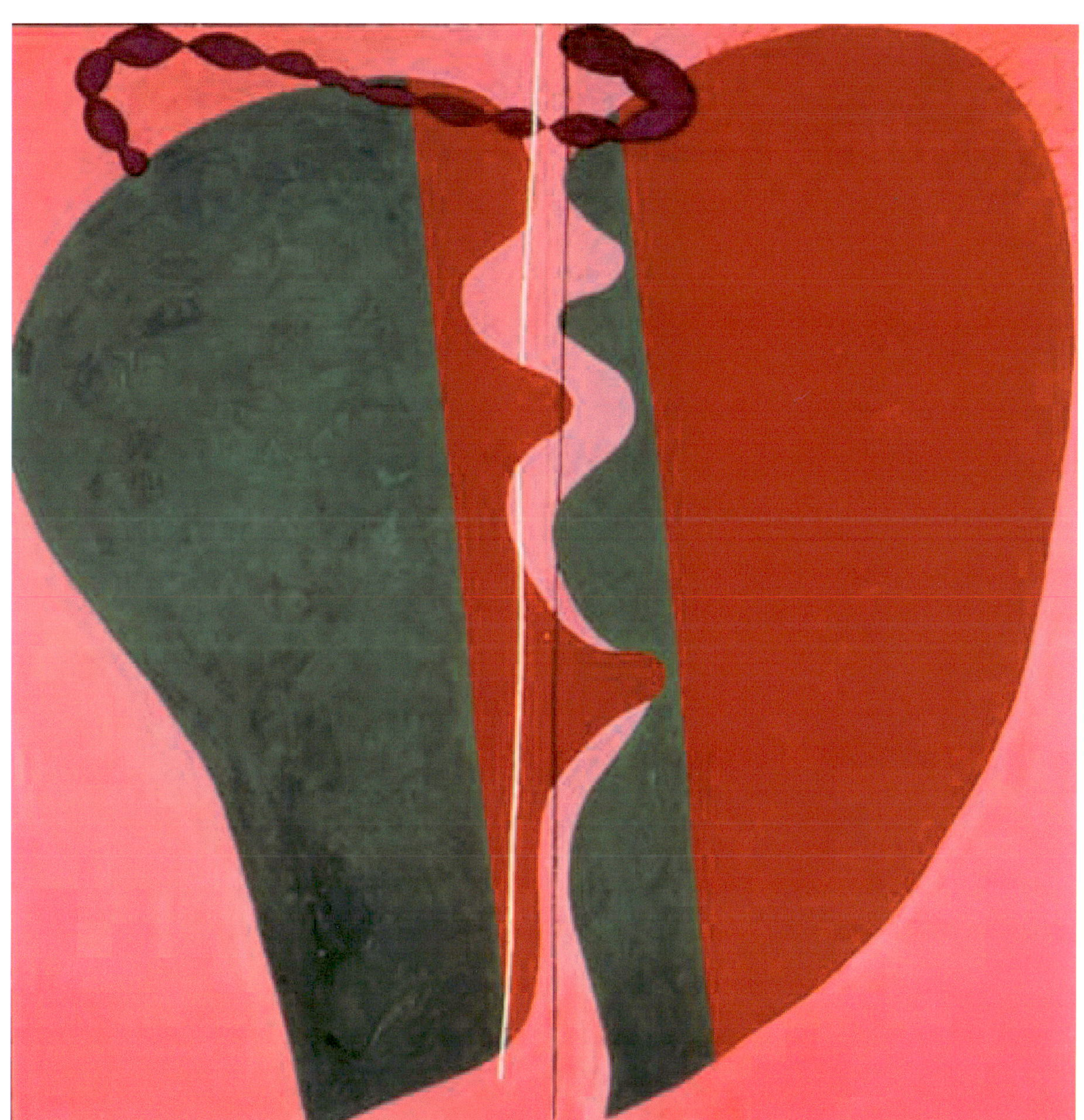

Kenneth NOLAND American, born 1924

Born in Asheville, North Carolina, Kenneth Noland began his career as a
Color Field painter. He experimented with shaped canvas painting, and, as
a result of an encounter with Helen Frankenthaler, also experimented with
staining unprimed canvases. Closely associated with the Hard-edge painters
such as Ellsworth Kelly, Noland did not change his style drastically over the
years, yet it remains difficult to categorize his work. Emphasizing the flatness
of the surface, Noland uses familiar forms like targets, flares and chevrons
to demonstrate the power of color and geometry. By using these simplified
forms, his focus is less on the subject and more on the formal relationships
between the shape of the canvas, the forms it contains, and the colors that
define these forms.

Mark is one of a series of paintings using chevrons and exemplifies all of
Noland's primary concerns. In works such as this, there is an emphasis
on the two-dimensional nature of a painting, which offers no sense of
illusionistic depth. S R

Mark, 1985
acrylic on canvas
89 x 79 ½ inches
Collection of Dr. J. Kenneth and Ellen T. Chance

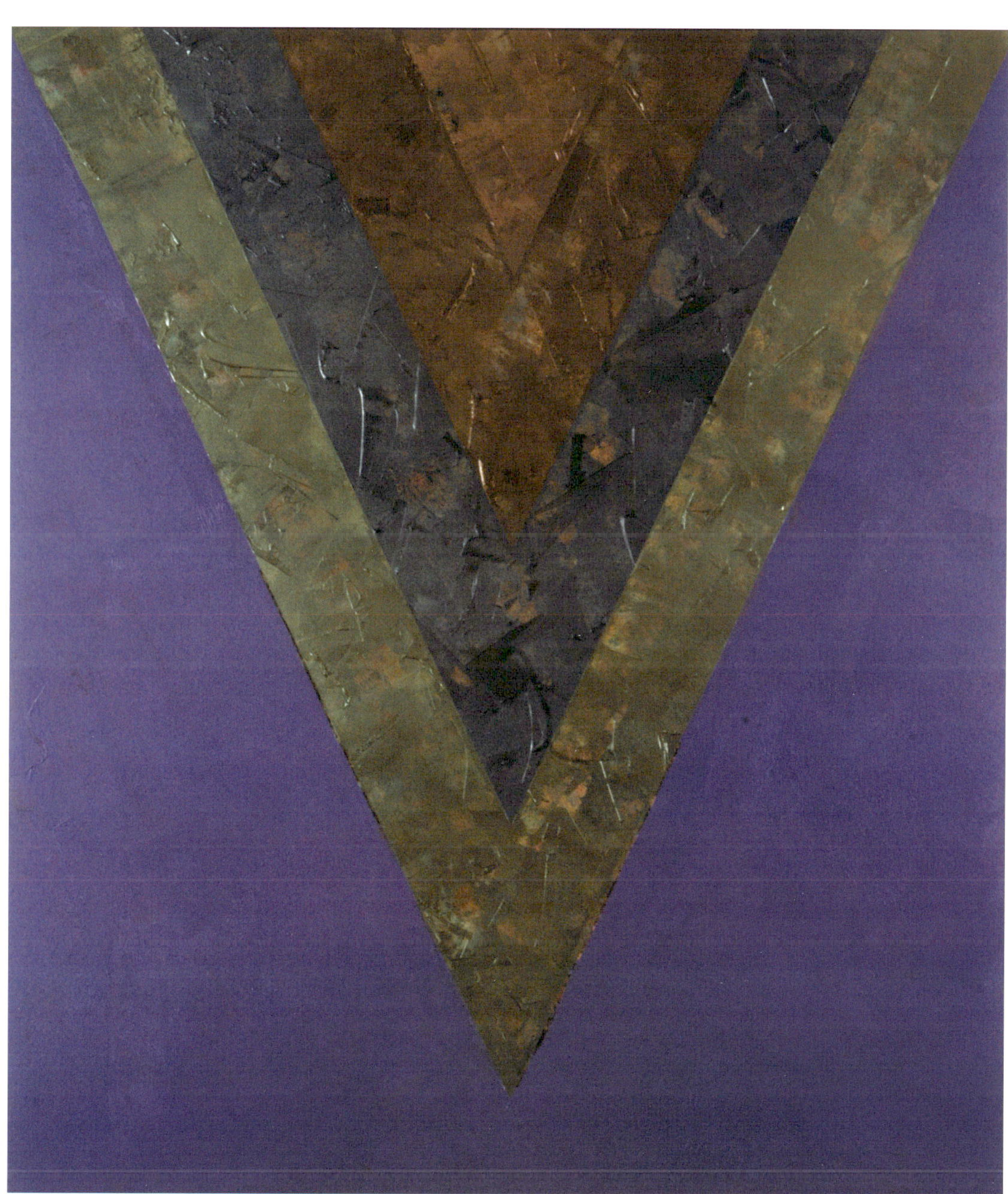

Deborah OROPALLO American, born 1954

Despite her recent exploration of the possibilities of digital media, Deborah Oropallo still considers herself a painter: "For me, the challenge within the tradition of painting is to derive contemporary meaning through the fusion of hand and mind, critical thinking as well as the use of common imagery and technology, to create something of measure or inspirational value."

Through the use of various media, Oropallo offers an inspiring, fresh look at seemingly mundane objects. *Snow White* is part of a series entitled *Stretch*. For this body of work, Oropallo finds her imagery on the Internet. By discovering and taking the images as they are, Oropallo has relinquished control over the lighting and the angle at which the pictures were taken. In this way, she herself becomes an observer who then finds new ways to present her subjects. In this particular image, she distorts an image of porcelain figurines of Snow White and the seven dwarfs, which she then further masks with a picket fence-like pattern. The underlying image is obscured, becoming a study in color and light. The uncomfortable and mysterious twisting of the familiar image, still faintly perceptible through the overlaying pattern, illuminates the artist's intent of showing the metaphorical dichotomies of the object: an apple may nourish or poison, or what can save you can also destroy you. L B

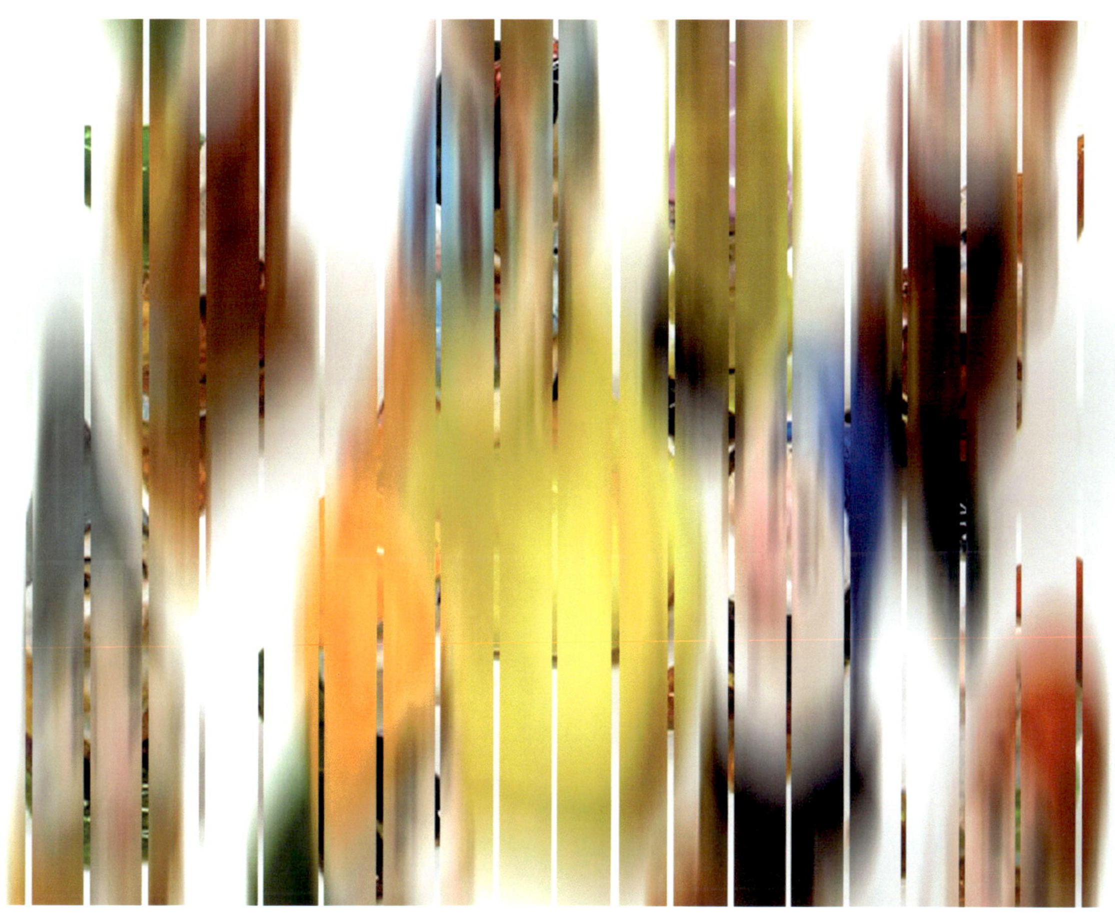

Snow White, 2005
inkjet on canvas printed in acrylic (edition 2/3)
57 x 77 inches
The Frank Konhaus and Ellen Cassilly Collection

Tony **OURSLER** American, born 1957

Tony Oursler has gained extensive fame for his haunting psychological video installations. Often dealing with issues of isolation, loneliness and angst, Oursler's work tests a viewer's ability to handle the range of emotions that his pieces often evoke, from fear and repulsion to humor and delight. In this work, *Invisible Green Link?*, from his 2007 series *Bluerialisation With Head*, Oursler experiments with the limits of his audio/video media. In all of the pieces in this series, LCD monitors are embedded into flat aluminum panels, which are cut and painted to mimic paint splatters. The artist then projects images of eyes or mouths onto the screens in blob-like shapes, which are sometimes accompanied by low mutterings or other sounds. By reversing the traditional roles of viewer and artwork, Oursler has created a painting that is no longer a stagnant object, but instead appears to be an animate entity that meets the gaze of the viewer and unabashedly stares back. L B

Invisible Green Link?, 2007
aluminum, acrylic, LCD screen, DVD player
57 x 61 x 4 $\frac{1}{2}$ inches
Collection of Randy Shull and Hedy Fischer
Courtesy of the Artist and Lehmann Maupin Gallery, New York

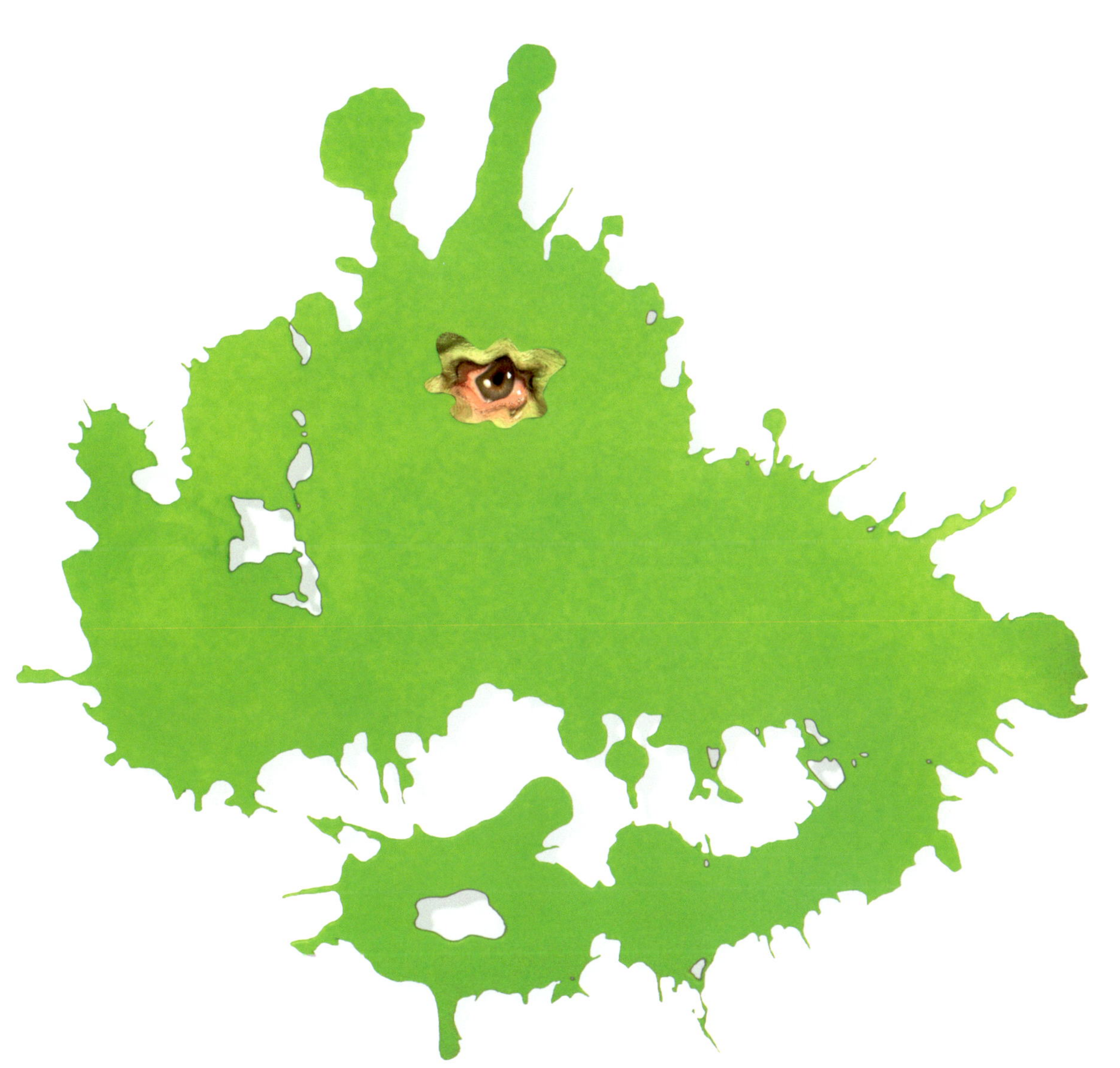

Nam June PAIK Korean, 1932-2006

Nam June Paik endeavored to humanize electronic media, a pursuit that was evident throughout his prolific, complex and visionary career. Trained as a musician and composer, Paik was uniquely capable of mining the temporal possibilities of the moving image. Recognizing TV's pervasiveness, Paik sought alternatives to its capacity to lull, entertain, persuade and make passive consumers of its audience. He set out to demystify the medium, and in doing so, transformed the video image into a tool capable of redefining the parameters of sculpture and installation art.

Paik's contribution is undeniable, now that time-based art informs much of our understanding of the visual arts in this new century. While some media artists focus on the optical, Paik embraced materiality as well as the ephemeral nature of technology. Meticulously editing an amalgam of pulsating visual images, Paik then arranged those images within a fabricated shell. *Dogmatic*, a humorous and thought-provoking sculpture, investigates the efficacy of the media to influence particular political, philosophical or moral beliefs. C M H

Dogmatic, 1996
two vintage television cabinets, one 13" color television,
one 8" color television, microphone, two vintage telephone
mouthpieces, one channel original Paik video, edition of 3
45 x 40 x 20 ½ inches
Collection of Renée and Paul Mansheim
Courtesy of Carl Solway Gallery, Cincinnati, Ohio

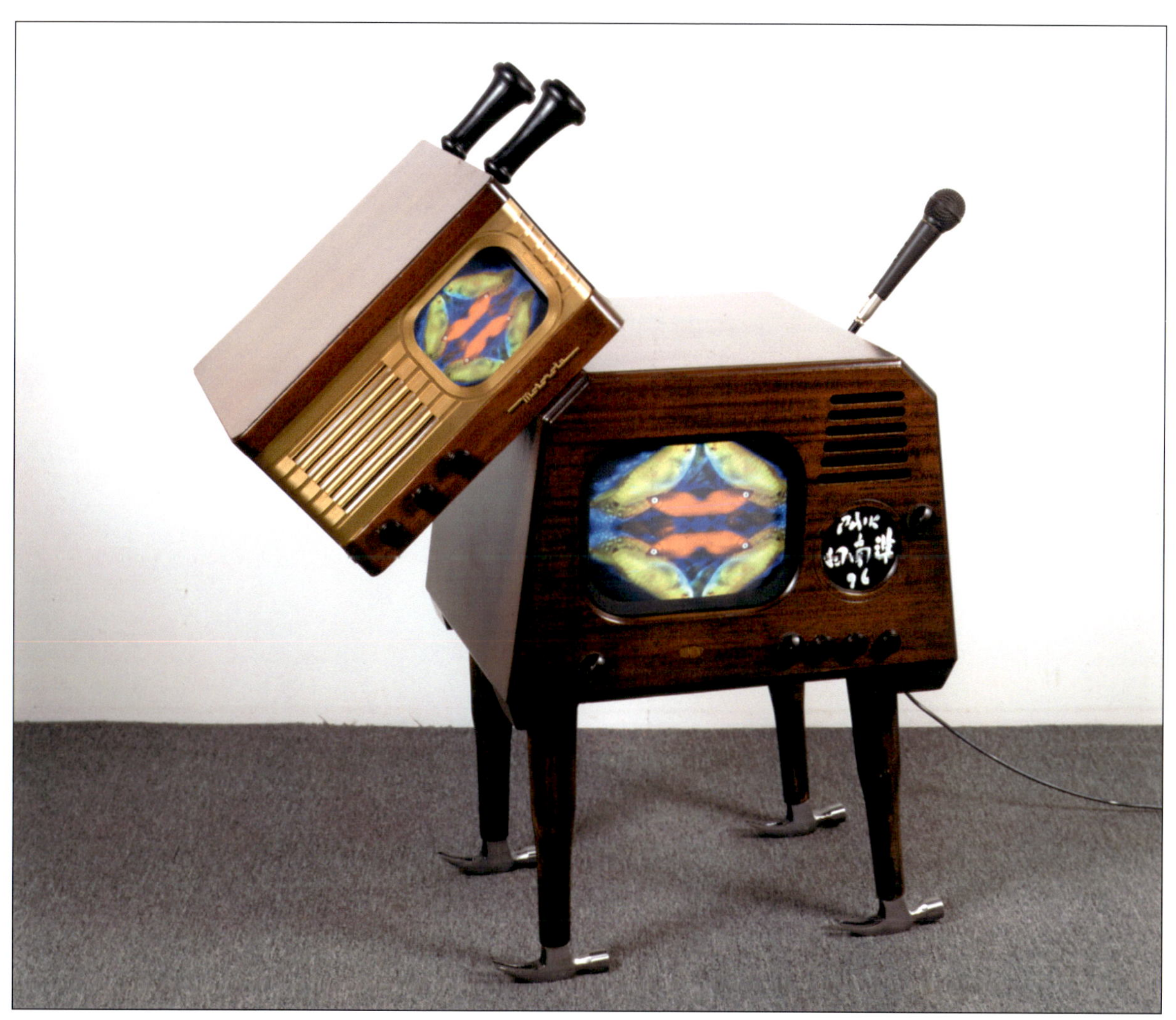

Robert and Shana PARKEHARRISON American, born 1968, 1964

The husband and wife duo of Robert and Shana ParkeHarrison have long been recognized for their black and white surrealist photographs, many of which examine the harm humankind has inflicted upon the natural world. Their elaborate scenes frequently center on an average, nameless figure, commonly known as Everyman; a persona who diligently, though sometimes futilely, works to "save and rejuvenate nature." Shana ParkeHarrison photographs Robert in various guises, and the resulting image is altered using a variety of techniques. Their most recent work, which includes color, continues to explore the relationships between mankind, nature and mortality. In *Mourning Cloak*, the brightly colored butterflies exude a life and vibrancy that is lacking in Everyman. This contrast might suggest that the butterflies act as a shield, protecting the character from his otherwise empty life, or perhaps that through interaction with the natural world we can lead a richer existence. L B

Mourning Cloak, 2006
photogravure (edition 1/4)
55 x 60 inches
Collection of Allen Thomas Jr., Wilson, North Carolina

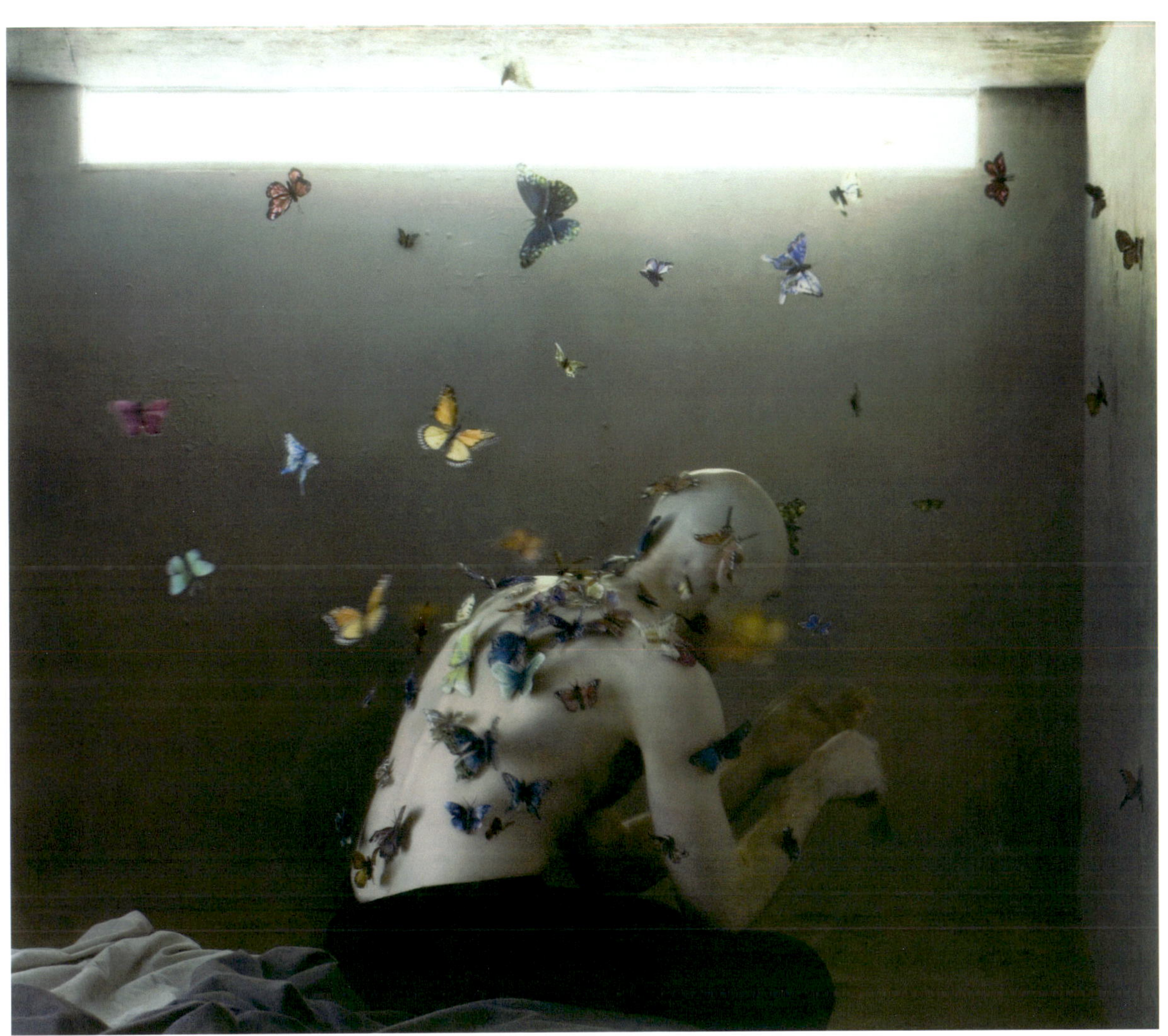

Judy Pfaff is best known for her large scale environments, or sculptural installations, a practice she began in the early 1970s. Although installation art was fairly marginal a few decades ago, it has become a central means of expression, in part because of Pfaff's pioneering practice. Throughout her career Pfaff has referenced the landscape, either through rather literal drawings or prints, or through the implied landscape of her sprawling and complex installations. *Old Night* is a panoramic rendering of a nocturnal, forested landscape which has been tinted a pale yellow. The print has been coated with a thin layer of beeswax and subsequently folded so that a grid of fine white lines is created. The landscape seems somewhat pristine and mysterious, but a tiny commercial sign implies that it has been circumscribed by inhabitants. The grid pattern also implies a commingling of the natural and the manufactured. Within this print one can see Pfaff's attempts to merge two antithetical visions of the American landscape. C M H

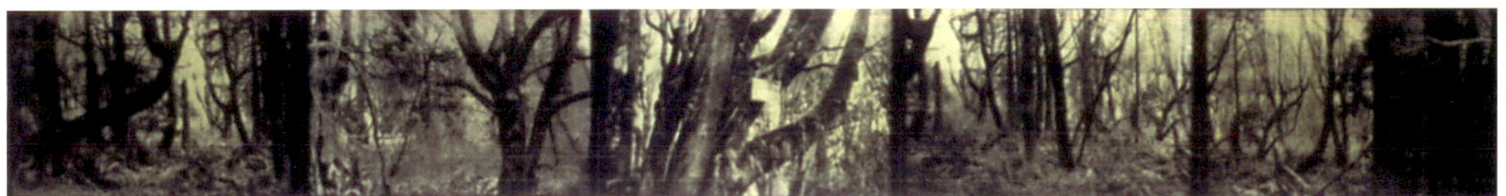

Old Night, 2000
photogravure, wax on Crown Kozo paper (edition 13/30)
8 ½ x 65 ½ inches
Collection of Doug Borwick and Julie Frye
Courtesy of Joie Lassiter Gallery

Sarah PICKERING   British, born 1972

London artist Sarah Pickering has forged a place for herself among the ranks of British landscape artists through her alteration of the traditionally serene expanses of the genre. The events photographed in her *Explosions* series, like the one seen in *Land Mine*, are based on media descriptions and eyewitness accounts of actual events, and designed with the help of a Hollywood pyrotechnic expert. Thus, the events themselves are formed by interpretation, and Pickering's photographs become comments on how media stories inform the public's perception of reality. Pickering describes her work as "a representation of society's coping mechanisms" in response to perceived threat and as looking at "fear and planning for the unexpected, merging fact and fiction, fantasy and reality." *Land Mine* also opens a dialogue on the distinction between what is real and what merely seems so, juxtaposing a violent, staged event with a serene pastoral setting. E B

116

Land Mine (from Explosions series), 2005
lambda print (edition 1/5)
49 x 49 inches
Collection of Allen Thomas Jr., Wilson, North Carolina
Courtesy of Daniel Cooney Fine Art, New York

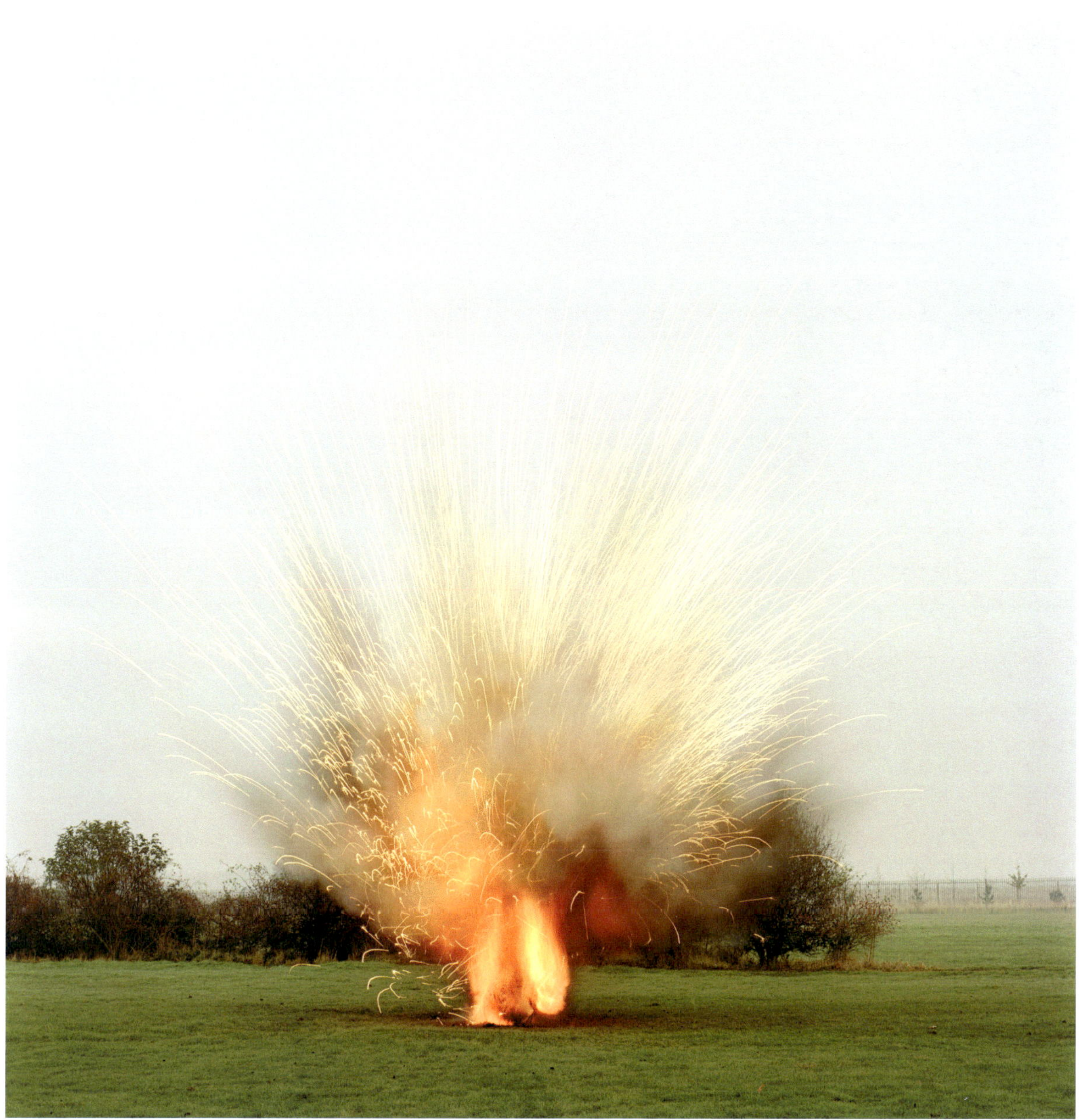

Liliana PORTER Argentinean, born 1941

Liliana Porter is interested in the relationship between things and their representations. *Drum Solo* is created entirely from found objects that Porter reappoints so that they shed their original identities and become conveyors of our own emotions and meanings. Employing her eclectic collection of knickknacks, toys and figurines, Porter creates a series of brief episodes and solo performances. Placed against neutral white or black backgrounds, these objects are animated by the artist through simple repositioning and abrupt changes of the camera's angle, while a gnomic musical score lends credibility to their frozen expressions and stilted motions. Porter's brilliant economy of means imbues these disparate figures with a poignant humanness and vulnerability.

The many-layered situations Porter devises within multiple episodes invite political, philosophical and existential interpretations. Pinned beneath a massive black shoe is a little boy; a tiny plastic soldier blasts a fat, smiling piggy bank; a bride and groom topple from a frothy, melting wedding cake. These kitschy characters evoke empathy and identification with the dramas they play out concerning universal themes of longing, loss and love. C M H

Drum Solo/Solo de Tambor, 2000
16 mm film transferred to digital video (19 minutes)
conceived and directed by Liliana Porter, music by Sylvia Meyer
Collection of Renée and Paul Mansheim
Exhibition copy: Courtesy of Liliana Porter

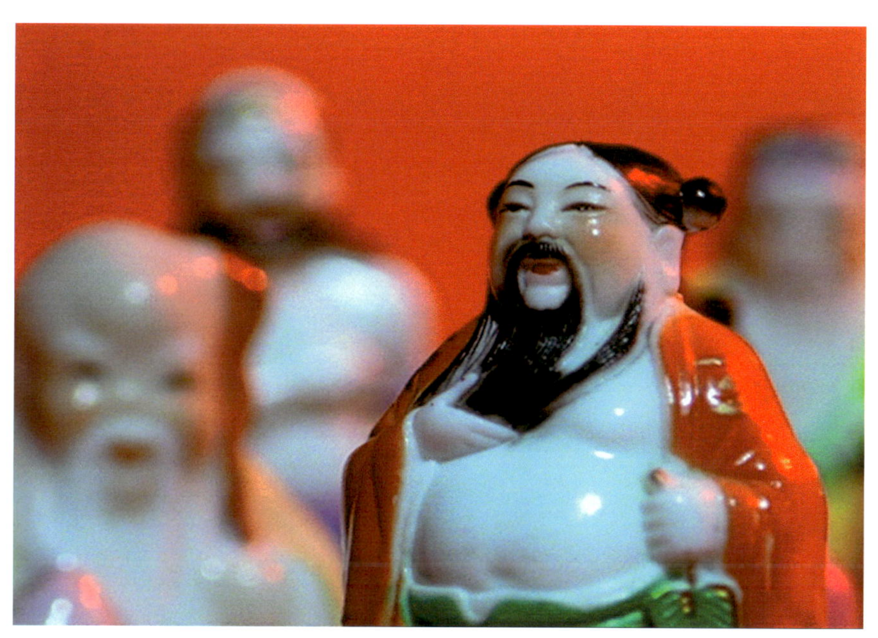

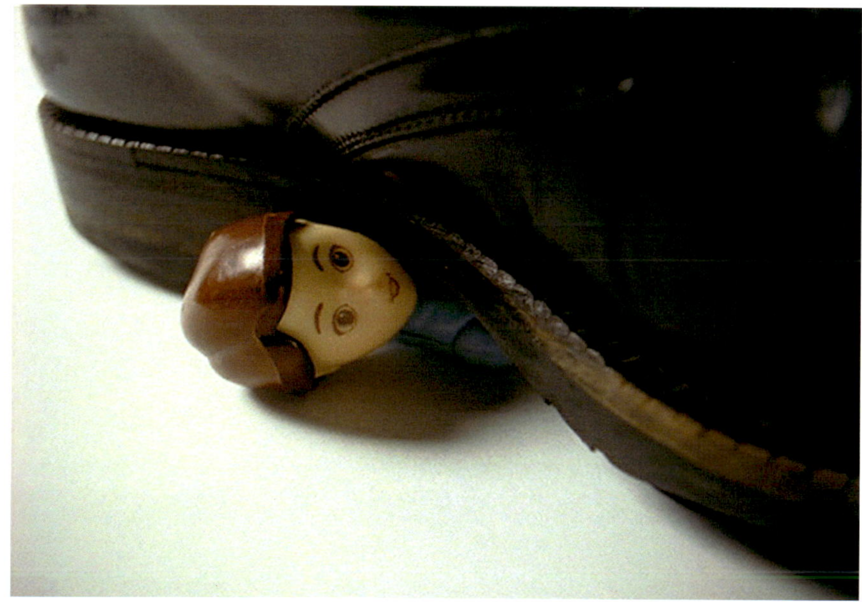

Michael PRINCE   American, born 1962

Michael Prince's carefully composed photograph of a girl in a bedroom in Westchester, New York, seems to evade placement in time. Without knowing the date of the photograph, it is difficult to pin down whether this image was created in the 1960s or in the present day. Kalia is represented through fragments: her face is not visible, but her clothing suggests that she is wearing a conservative school uniform. Given equal billing with the girl is an old rabbit-eared TV, its screen broadcasting scratchy static. The room's faded floral wallpaper creates an eerie quality. Within this composition are many circular motifs ranging from the wooden dresser's knobs and medallions, to the TV's control knobs, to the single button on Kalia's navy blue skirt. The child's pale knees and hands lend a fragile quality to this mysterious portrait, perhaps suggesting the fragility of both childhood and memory. C M H

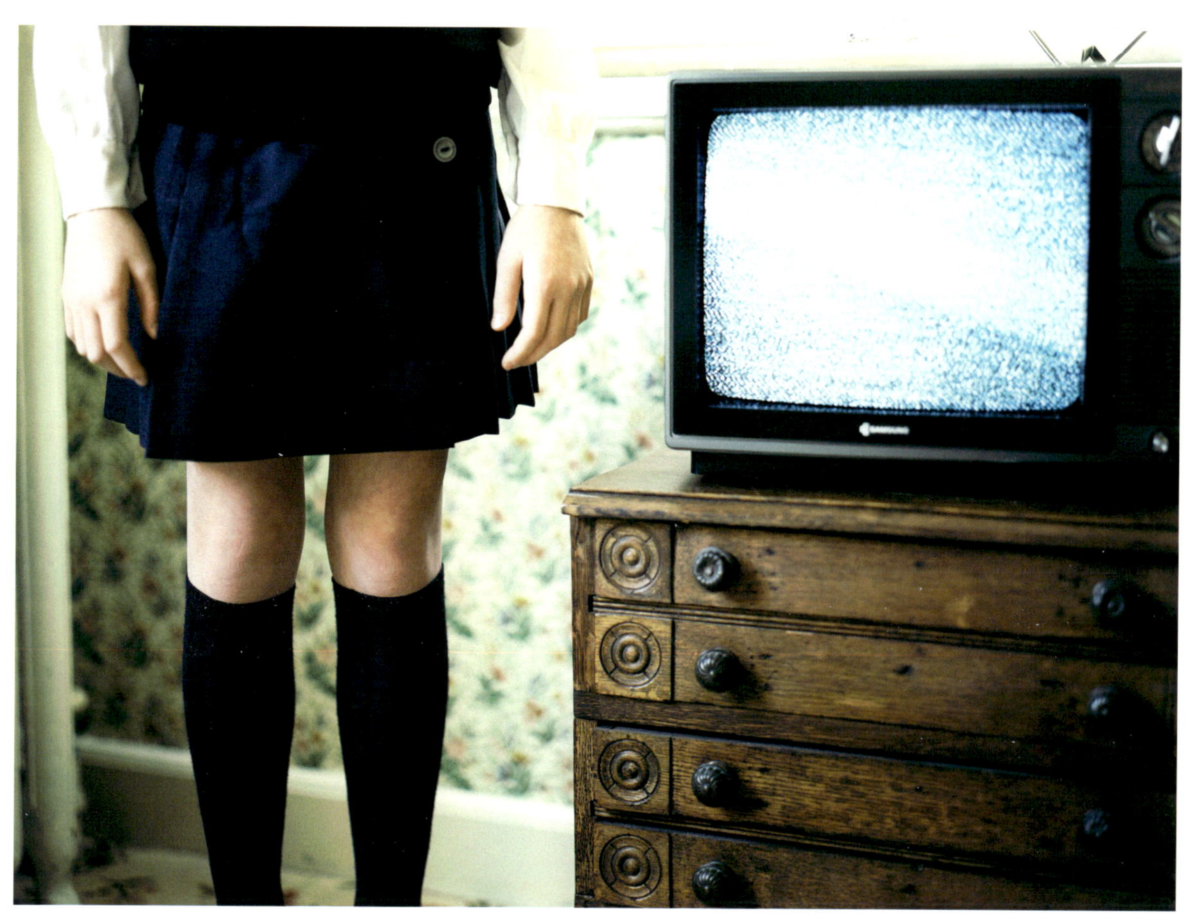

Kalia and TV Westchester 2002, 2002
c-print (edition 5/10)
30 x 39 inches
The Frank Konhaus and Ellen Cassilly Collection

Stephanie PRYOR American, born 1971

Stephanie Pryor's buoyant abstractions are comprised of fluid shapes, spills and splashes that meander across a flat eggshell surface. *Untitled (painting light blue background)* reveals an unconventional yet balanced composition of billowy shapes and delicate lines that perhaps allude to a menagerie of aquatic creatures. Pryor prepares a sanded wood panel with many layers of gesso, then applies acrylic paint and ink in quick, sweeping pours and gestures. The translucent quality of the media lends her paintings a delicacy—the voluminous forms seem to float above the surface, as though suspended in a watery realm. The semi-recognizable shapes within Pryor's painting easily sink back into the plane of the nonspecific. Palpable tension is created within this painting by juxtaposing the vibrant physicality of the liquid passages with the flat, opaque areas, offsetting the sensual vigor with hard-edged control. C M H

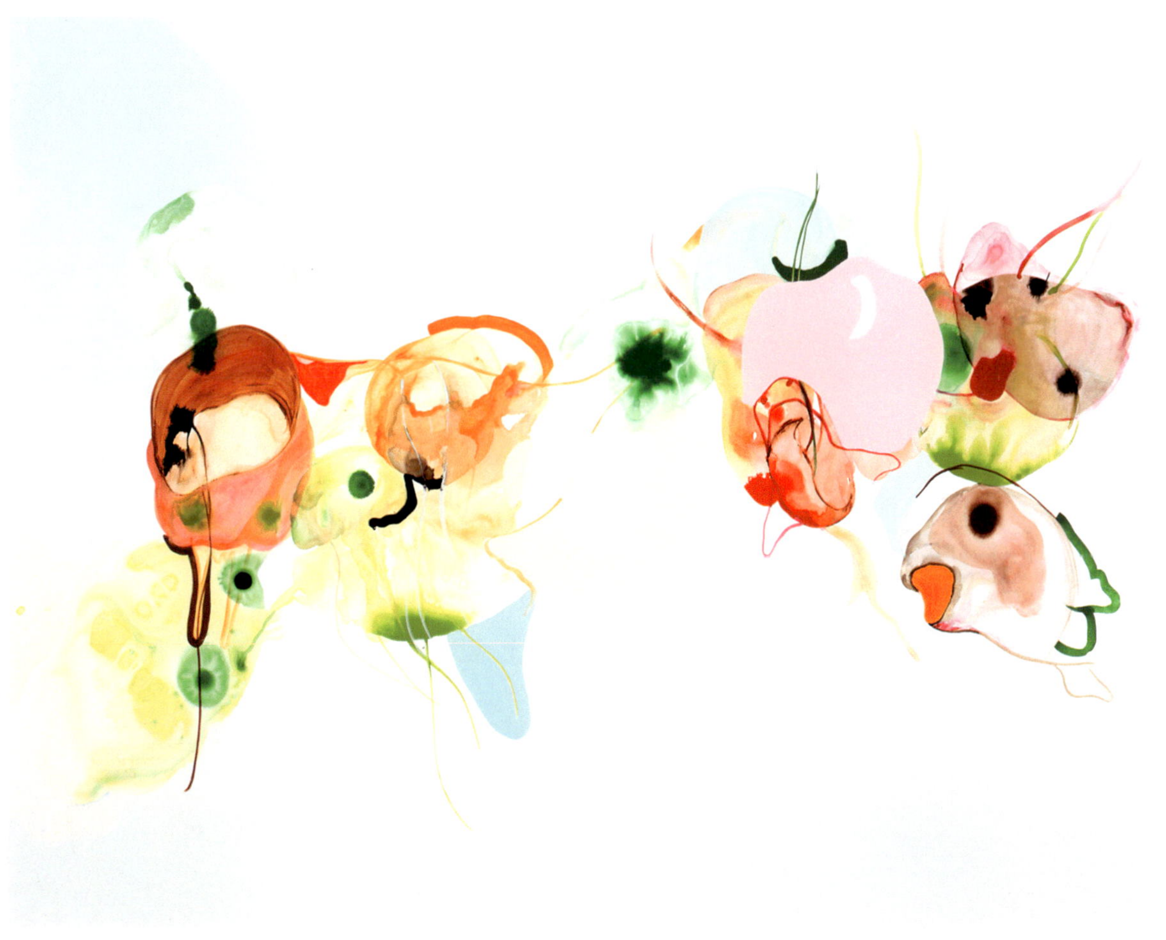

123

Untitled (painting light blue background), 2000
acrylic paint and acrylic ink on gessoed board
48 x 72 inches
Collection of Paul and Sara Monroe

Susan ROTHENBERG American, born 1945

In the early 1970s Susan Rothenberg was among several young New York artists who began to create representational paintings as a reaction against the reductive, often geometric paintings of the late 1960s. She became known for iconic paintings of horses, which acted as a personal symbol and became the means for Rothenberg to explore a range of expressive, formalist and narrative concerns. In the late 1980s Rothenberg began to include the human figure (or fragments of the figure) in her paintings, a motif that she continues to explore in her most recent paintings.

Smoke Rings uses highly simplified figurative fragments—a white arm is draped across the back of a red sofa, while at the upper edge of the canvas a black finger pierces one of five floating smoke rings. This potent imagery is not easily deciphered, but suggests an intimate connection between the two individuals who are referenced but not entirely revealed. According to Rothenberg she utilizes a strategy of "displacing things and putting them back together in a way that is partly intuitive." CMH

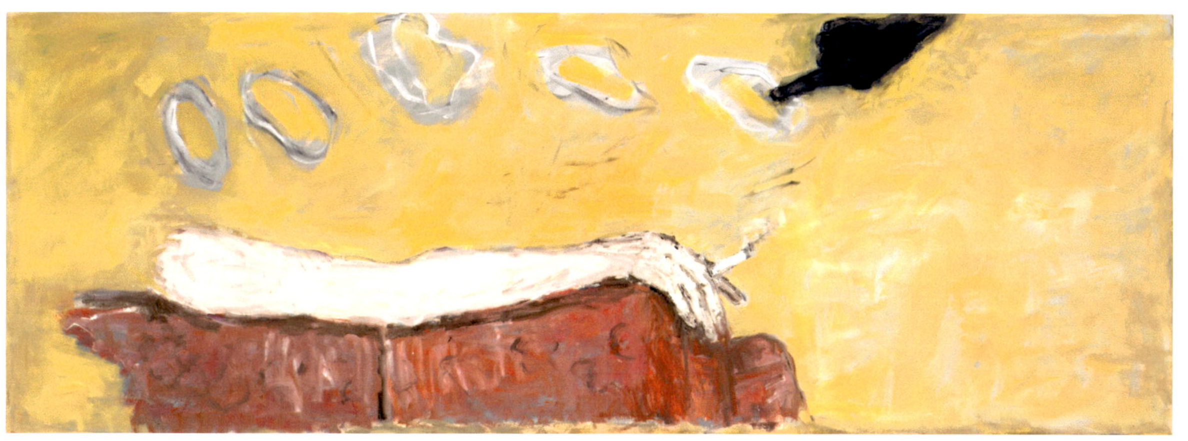

Smoke Rings, 2003
oil on canvas
35 x 100 inches
Collection of Randy Shull and Hedy Fischer
Courtesy of Sperone Westwater, New York

Michal ROVNER Israeli, born 1957

For the 50th Venice Biennale, Israeli artist Michal Rovner created *DataZone* (2003), a stunning and provocative installation. Viewers entered a mysterious, darkened space containing rows of long tables that were embedded with illuminated Petri dishes. Upon closer inspection, it was revealed that these dishes contained miniscule videos of figures wearing black robes and head coverings. Dancing within the confines of the perimeters, these individuals silently move against a stark, white background. A product of painstaking digital editing, Rovner's intimately scaled videos bring into focus the spare beauty of humanity from a bird's-eye perspective.

While some may view this work as political commentary, especially in the context of Rovner's life in Israel, she prefers a more open interpretation without specific narratives. Freezing the lyrical movements of the figures in the diminutive video, *Culture #4* is created from a still of Rovner's transfixing installation. C M H

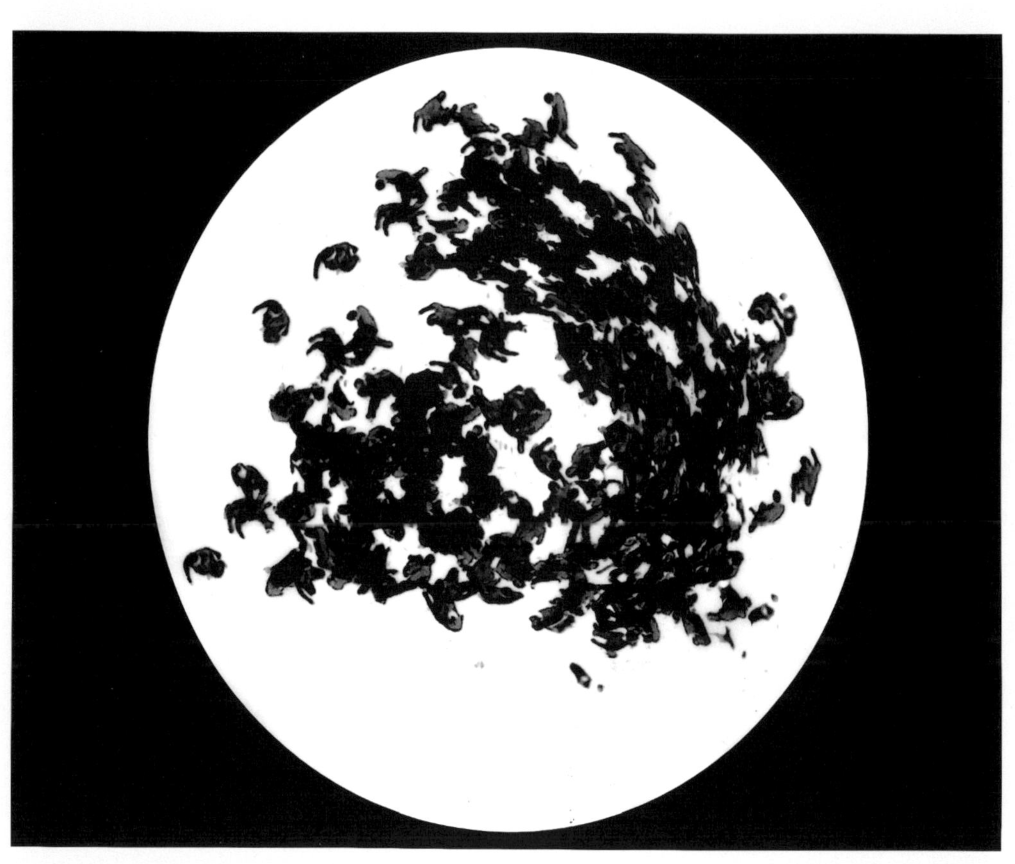

Culture #4, 2003
pure pigment on archival paper (edition 3/6)
37 ¼ x 54 ½ inches
Collection of Renée and Paul Mansheim

Alison SAAR American, born 1956

As the child of mixed heritage artists, Alison Saar is extremely cognizant of the powers of both art and race. Her mother, Betye Saar, is of African, Native American and European heritage, while her father is of European descent. With a strong interest in artistic and folkloric representations of racial stereotypes, Alison Saar has long used found objects, including tin, wood and metal, to create sculptures that attest to the strong spiritual connection she feels with both the objects and her diverse heritage. *Rise Sally Rise* was part of a 2003 exhibition entitled "Lost/Found" and explores the idea of change. Created at a time when Saar's daughter was moving into adolescence and her son into pre-adolescence, the piece shows an adolescent girl sitting in a chair too small for her developing body. As she leans over the chair, perched precariously both on the edge of the wall and adulthood, her hair mingles with bottles as it falls toward the floor. L B

128

Rise Sally Rise, 2003
mixed media
54 x 34 x 14 inches
Collection of Randy Shull and Hedy Fischer

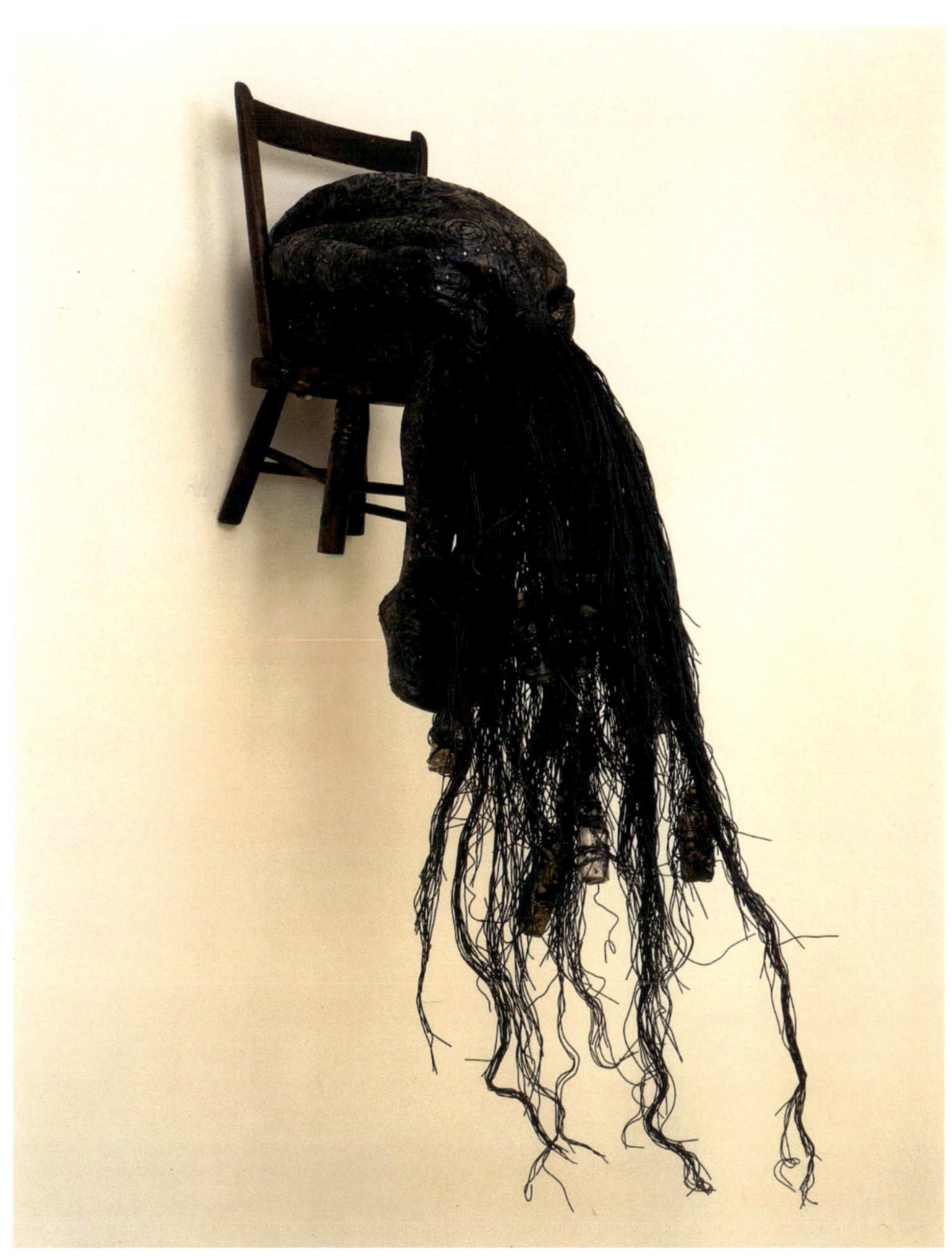

Tom SACHS American, born 1966

Tom Sachs' bricolage sculptures explore ideas about consumerism while simultaneously commenting on religion and politics. Sachs remains a controversial figure in the art world because of his subject matter and his appropriation of copyrighted material (which ranges from a "Hello Kitty Nativity" to a "Prada Death Camp"). Intermingling high and low art in his handmade sculptures, Sachs often uses cheap and commonplace materials like foam-cor to create works that wryly comment on rampant consumerism, which he believes creates a bland, homogenized culture. Sachs' sculptures can be seen as both rejecting this loss of culture and embracing it.

Sachs' most recent sculptures are foreboding assemblages that point to a dystopian future. *FBH* is part of his *post-apocalyptic furniture* series. This self-contained furnishing, like a home-spun curiosity cabinet, contains supplies for when the world comes to an end: cans of beans, cigarettes, a bottle of whiskey and a gun, among other necessary provisions. Part humorous, part sinister, the meanings contained within this work are varied and complex. S R

FBH, 2006
mixed media
55 x 55 x 24 inches
Collection of Randy Shull and Hedy Fischer
Courtesy of the Artist and Galerie Thaddaeus Ropac

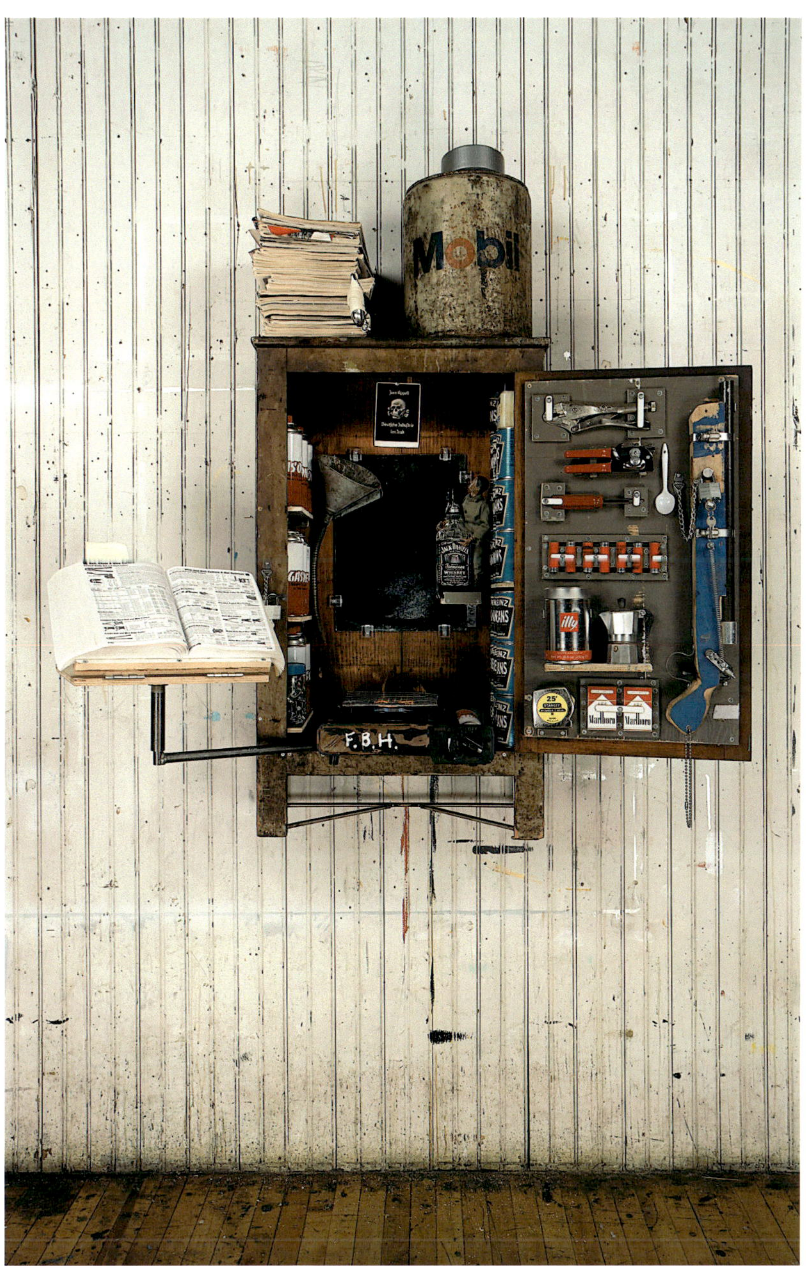

Lorna SIMPSON American, born 1960

Beginning her career as a documentary photographer, Lorna Simpson soon realized that all of her photographs would be interpreted by a viewer according to their own background and personal culture. In order to rectify this problem, Simpson began to photograph fragments of black women—their backs, torsos and arms—intentionally concealing their faces, then added a series of words to direct the viewer's thoughts to her own interpretations. Simpson's 1991 journey to the South to produce a piece for the Spoleto Festival in Charleston, South Carolina, had a deep impact on her. This work, *Counting*, was created in the aftermath of that experience. The central photograph in this group depicts a circular hut from Boone Hall Plantation. The phrase "1575 bricks" printed beside it alludes to the number of bricks that make up the building, which was likely constructed by black slaves. The round shape of the hut suggested to the artist the circularity of a woman's neckline as well as a popular hairstyle: a coiffure of braids. The twisted hair may suggest the age of the woman, representing the multitude of experiences she has had over her lifetime. L B

132

Counting, 1991
photogravure with screenprinting
73 ¾ x 38 inches
Collection of Jean Crutchfield and Robert Hobbs

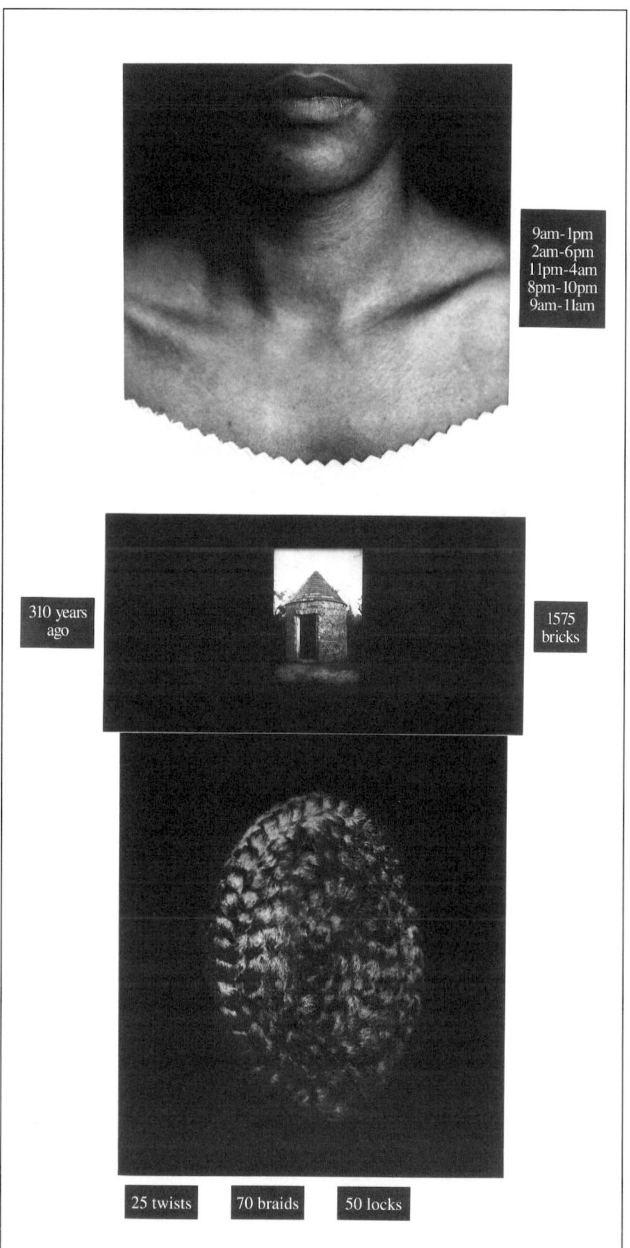

9am-1pm
2am-6pm
11pm-4am
8pm-10pm
9am-11am
310 years
ago
1575
bricks
25 twists
70 braids
50 locks

Donald SULTAN American, born 1951

Donald Sultan was born in Asheville, North Carolina, and has become renowned for his innovative abstraction of traditional still life subjects. His brightly colored fruits, dominos and flowers—such as The Mint Museums' *Aqua Poppies*—pop against dark backgrounds, their stylized forms balanced by an underlying grid structure. Where a writer might assign an inorganic object its own personality, Sultan reverses the process, sterilizing natural forms by cutting them into vinyl squares mounted on Masonite and filled with plaster and tar. The intriguing contrast of unwieldy, nontraditional materials with graceful organic subjects has brought much attention to his work.

His series of smoke ring prints, including *Smoke Rings January 12, 2001*, replaces these kinds of juxtapositions with another – here the free forms of white smoke rings, which float against black backgrounds within the strict geometric confines of the sheet of paper that they are printed upon. Sultan compensates for the physical flatness of the photograph by creating a vast sense of space within and around the swirling shapes. E B

134

Smoke Rings January 12, 2001, 2001
digital inkjet print (HC 1)
34 x 34 inches
Collection of Cheryl Walker and Jeff Huberman

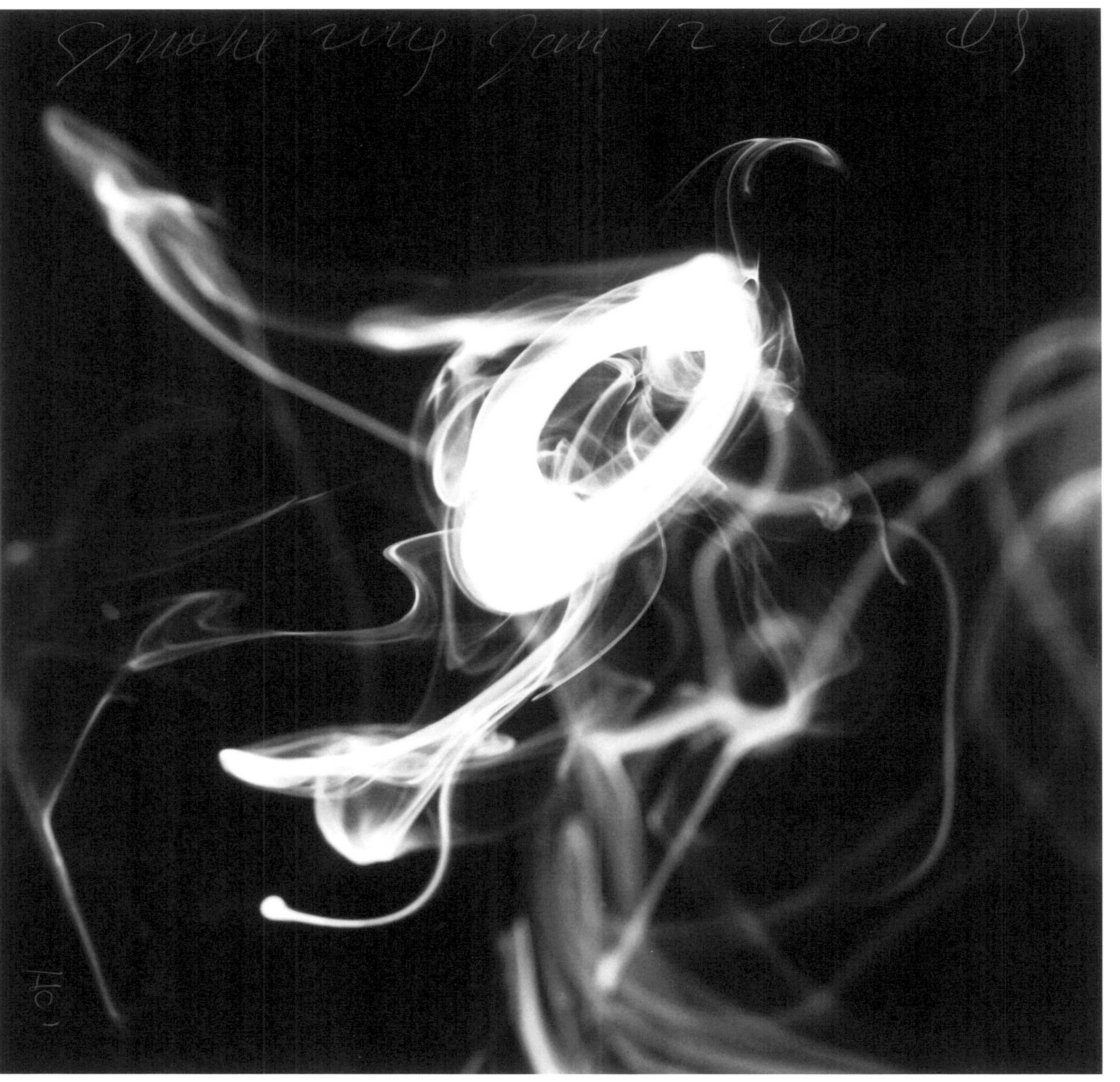

Smoke ring Jan 12 2001 DS

Mark TANSEY American, born 1949

Since the late 1970s Mark Tansey has been investigating the rich possibilities of content conveyed through monochromatic paintings that make coherent connections between disparate ideas and events. "In contrast to the assertion of one reality, my work investigates how different realities interact and abrade," he says. Tempestuous waves heave a tiny ship in Tansey's collage, *Columbus Discovers Spain*, which serves as a study for a painting of the same title. At the upper right corner, mysterious arches suggest an improbable swimming pool ladder.

It is significant that this work was created in 1992, which marked the quincentennial of Columbus' discovery of America. This discovery resulted not only in the colonization of the continent but also the demise of many indigenous cultures. Tansey uses irony and surrealistic combinations to allude as well to the skeptical reception Columbus received upon returning to Spain. This composition suggests a collapsing of time and space—the Atlantic Ocean shrinks to a swimming pool, and the relativity and ramifications of Columbus' discovery are examined as it telescopes across centuries. C M H

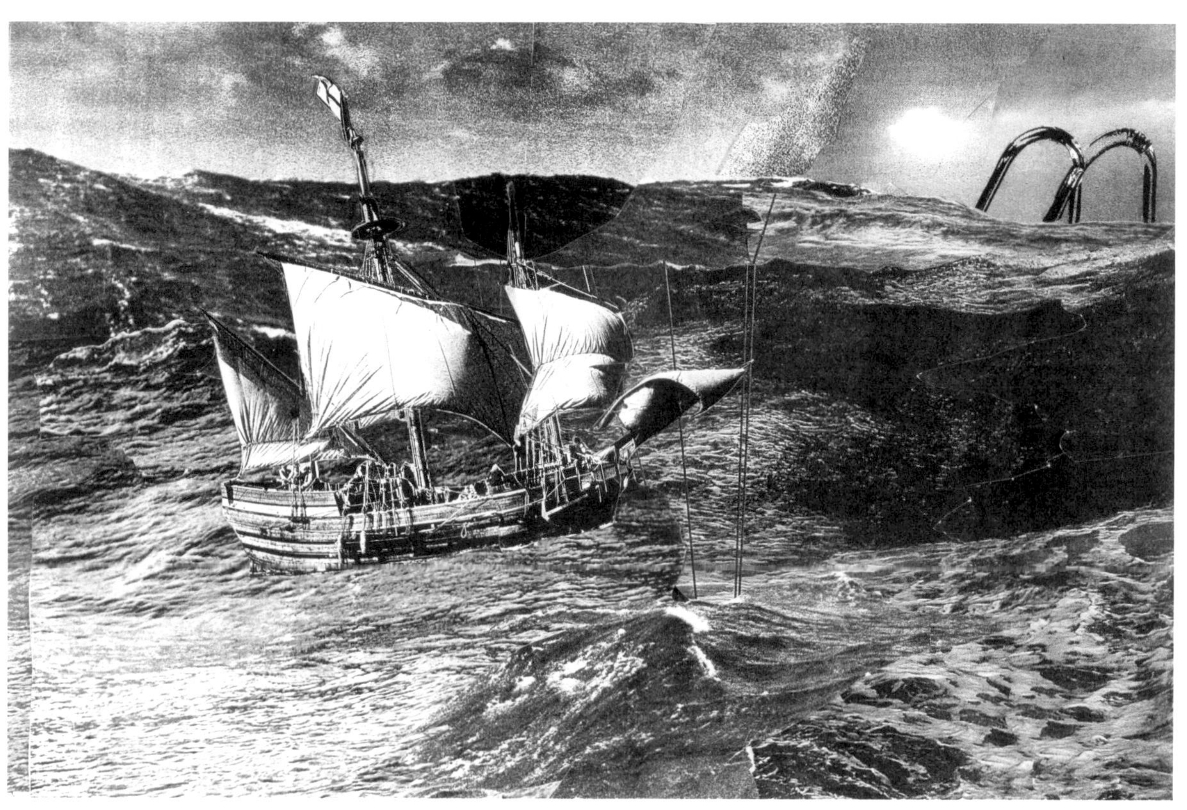

Columbus Discovers Spain, 1992
collage
12 x 16 ¼ inches
Collection of Annabel Manning and Michael Kelly

Mark TOBEY American, 1890-1976

A member of the Northwest Mystics group, Mark Tobey enjoyed an artist's community with Kenneth Callahan, Morris Graves and Guy Anderson during the Depression in Seattle. Tobey taught himself the tenets of artistic expression through salon discussions with his friends. In the 1930s, Tobey emerged from the dreary palette favored by that group, blending it with the influence of Asian bronzes and calligraphy to develop a kind of "white writing"—a web of white lettering that he layered over urban iconography. Inspired by his travels, readings of Eastern philosophy, and conversion to the Bahá'í faith, Tobey imparted balance and unity to his works. Merging East and West, science and religion, he worked towards symbolizing the human spirit and oneness of the world. *Flame of Colors*, from the *Homage to Tobey Portfolio*, exemplifies Tobey's move towards pure abstraction, in which interwoven calligraphic marks represent universal methods of communication, replacing written words with painted gestures. E B

Flame of Colors (from the *Homage to Tobey* portfolio), 1974
lithograph PP
25 ½ x 29 ¾ inches
Collection of Thomas E. Kanes and Susan Valentine Kanes

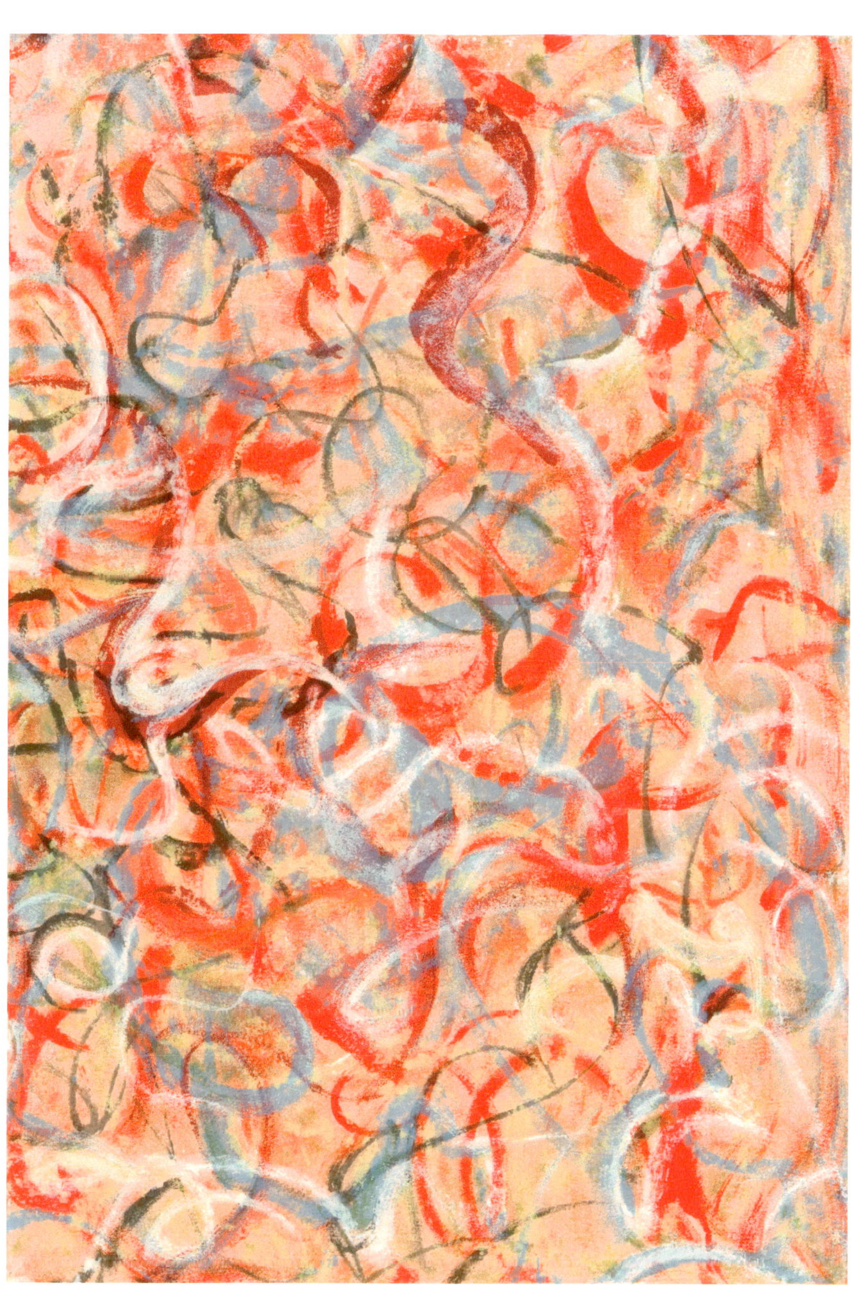

Kara WALKER   American, born 1970

The art of silhouettes has long been considered a way of rendering emotionless, innocent portraits for a white, middle-class America. It was this notion that attracted Kara Walker to the silhouette form as she sought a way to portray her quest for identity as a black woman through the exploration of antebellum racial stereotypes. Most commonly seen in large-scale installations, often with overhead projectors adding colored lights to the scene (as well as projecting the shadows of viewers directly into the image), Walker's work has caused some to become enthralled with the beauty of her craft and others to be appalled by her unflinching representation of racism in America. Walker welcomes both kinds of reactions. While she is on a quest to uncover herself and her roots, she hopes that viewers, too, will be forced to look at themselves and face their own prejudices and fears: "You look or you don't look. But I'll make it as long as I have to." L B

I'll be a Monkey's Uncle, 1995
lithograph (edition 1/25)
39 ½ x 35 inches
Collection of Jean Crutchfield and Robert Hobbs

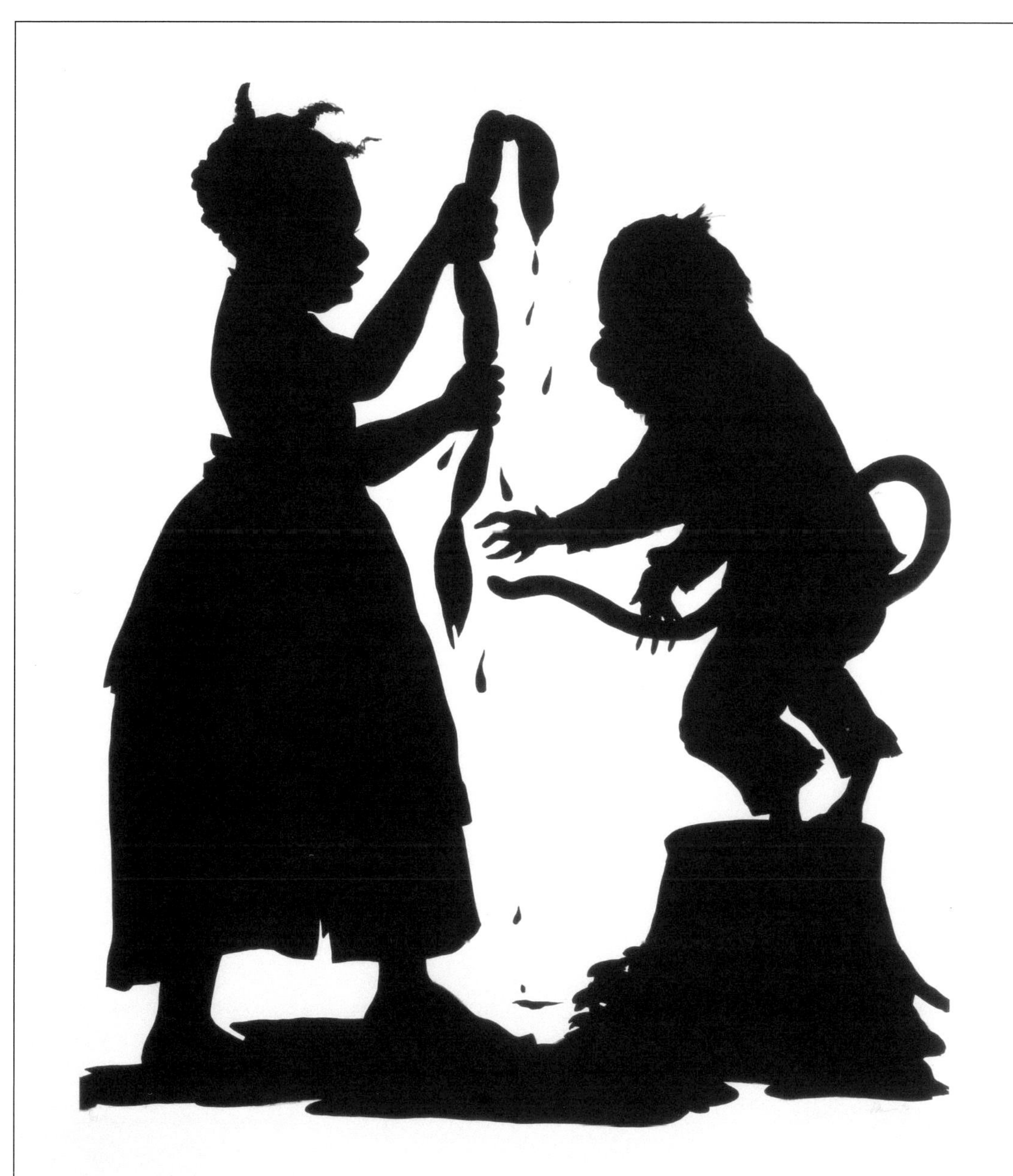

Friendships with artists have been a big part of my collecting; going to galleries, art fairs and museum shows with working artists has given me confidence in my eye. Certain art causes in me an almost physically joyous reaction. Luckily, the artists I know produce considerable and diverse work I find really moving. So, having limited resources, I only buy art of artists I know. My collection thereby gives me both visual pleasure as well as memories of the individuals who created it.

Adrián Halpern

We can't imagine living any other way. We love work that we don't always understand; it challenges us and is refreshing on a daily basis. Sometimes collecting is like a scavenger hunt but without a list.

Randy Shull & Hedy Fischer

I collect contemporary art because it allows me to make a commitment to the ideas expressed and to the artists who make the work. It is a very different intellectual pursuit than my everyday occupation as a physician. I love the evaluation of new work that hasn't yet been validated by curators and critics. Trying to figure out what new work will continue to inspire keeps my mind open and flexible.

Paul Monroe

We choose works of art based on both visual attraction and historic relevance. Living with art provides the opportunity to be constantly inspired by each work.

Thomas E. Kanes and **Susan Valentine Kanes**

Goethe said, "A person should see … a fine picture every day in order that worldly cares may not obliterate the sense of the beautiful which God has implanted in the human soul."

This sentiment expressed so articulately has been a stimulus in our building a collection of paintings, drawings, sculptures, glass and clay, which we feel enriching our lives daily.

From the teen years onward, fostered by visits to museums and galleries here and abroad, the foundation was prepared for the eventual formation of a collection, each piece with a story associated.

We have been guided along the way by artists, gallery owners, museum directors, curators, and volumes of books and monographs—each adding a different perspective on our appreciation of things collected.

Our interests are protean but our collection over the past 25 years has tended to fall into three categories: North Carolina art, Bay Area work principally from the '40s to the '60s, and the Color Field movement. We have been fortunate enough to meet many of the artists in our collection, which adds a great dimension.

We have come to love many of the pieces in our collection—they almost seem like family members rather than inanimate objects. Having lived with them day to day, we always like the idea of sharing them with others and welcome any opportunity to make them available for enjoyment and education.

Our first major art purchase was of a 1930s landscape and figurative work by eastern North Carolina native Francis Speight, who taught for many years at the Pennsylvania Academy of Fine Arts and who started the studio art department at UNC-Chapel Hill. He frequently served as juror with Thomas Hart Benton. We next collected a small Benton oil painting, which pushed us to a whole different level and widened our scope. From there, it has been a very enjoyable and educational experience to assimilate our pieces.

We particularly like the five pieces that we are loaning for this exhibition. We never grow tired of gazing at the impressive, elegant, colorful abstraction *Denominator* by Helen Frankenthaler. It is one of the largest pieces in our collection and the focal piece of our Tall Room at home. The smaller, whimsical *The Fourth*, signed "Independently Yours," and created around a July 4th holiday, is lyrical and energetic. Noland's *Mark* is magnificently precise and textural—a variation of his seminal '60s works. The Anthony Caro is very powerful for a table piece and the assemblage of cast bronzes is harmonious and balanced. Anderson's piece, one of our favorites, is sleek, sensual and magical—exciting from any viewing angle. The impeccably smooth surface is perfect.

Collecting works created from the imagination, creativity and genius of various artists has been a great part of our lives and has continued with our grown children as well. It is gratifying to realize that they are building their own collections in their early adulthood having valued growing up surrounded with original works of art.

Ken Chance

I suspect collecting art is somehow rooted in my DNA. From an early age, I found myself hoarding things of interest: small ceramic statues, stamps, postcards, dinosaur trading cards, beads.

I was a fairly bad art student, but found my way around the classroom culling through other people's works. Ultimately, I would try (and succeed) in purchasing some of the work—and that's when I fell feet first into collecting contemporary art. I instantly got over the urge to produce art, and realized acquiring it was more my thing.

After college, I was introduced to contemporary photography at a gallery in New Orleans—and have been hooked ever since. It's been an evolution, starting with black and white photography that has progressed to large scale color work, and beyond. I've learned to never say never, as my tastes are wide, and somewhat fluid. I struggle to find a focus in the collection as a whole, and since I never collected that way, lack of obvious themes is not surprising.

Never lost in the process is the artist, though, and there is some appeal to helping support and encourage artists who are full of passion about what they do. I can get just as caught up in an artist, as a piece of art, but ultimately—I love (visually) everything I'm lucky enough to drag home. Again, it's in my DNA.

Allen Thomas Jr.

Surrounding ourselves with works of art, particularly photographic portraits, that surprise, engage, and nourish us, has become as essential as food and shelter.

There is an immediacy, a contemporary quality, and a simple graphic allure to photography that compels like no other medium for us. Ours is a collection as much of images as it is of stories. Many of the photographers we collect and gallery owners we patronize have become friends and most of our photographs are tightly bound to a story of discovery or a particularly wonderful art fair or travel destination. We are not focused on technique or process and frankly cannot identify a unifying theme, but the group works and evolves well as a collection.

We enjoy the role of amateur curator in our home discovering new relationships and connections as we make new groupings of images. An unusual fascination for us is the bond formed in the impromptu micro communities comprised of common holders of a single limited edition image. Much of the collection lives at my office and it has been a particular treat seeing my clients and employees, some who have had limited exposure to fine art, migrate from mild bafflement to almost possessiveness about certain pieces.

Frank Konhaus

I have been collecting art since I was an undergraduate college student. My first purchase was a re-strike copy of a William Hogarth lithograph titled *Beer Street*. It is not difficult to understand why an undergraduate male student, taking summer courses at the University of Wisconsin in Madison, would find such a print to be of interest.

A few years later, in 1973, Renée and I took our first trip together outside of North America. We went to London. On Portobello Road we found a set of *Marriage á la Mode* and the series was actually printed in Hogarth's lifetime. We discovered the importance of documentation when we were fortunate enough to secure a copy of Paulson's catalog of Hogarth engravings. We were able to tell the exact date of each lithograph. The lithographs were in their original Regency frames and even the glass was original.

In the 1980s, we became interested in the plight of Jews living in the Soviet Union who were not allowed to leave. We made three visits to the former Soviet Union. We thought perhaps it would be interesting to get involved in the "unofficial" art of the Soviet Union. We discovered that one of the artists that attracted us, Mihail Chemiakin, had a lot of tribal themes in his art. From there we became interested in tribal art and have collected a couple of hundred pieces of African Art, mainly from Nigeria.

Having learned that tribal art was an important influence on contemporary art, we subsequently went on to become interested in abstraction, but also in the influence of Marcel Duchamp. From here it was not a stretch to be interested in Nam June Paik, in photography, in video, and in a wide variety of creative expression.

About 10 or so years ago, I went to a lecture by Suzi Gablik, in which she explored "environmental art." I don't think I understood too much of what she said at the time that I heard her talk, but I suspect a seed was planted in my unconscious to be receptive to the work of Andy Goldsworthy.

Some of the works in our collection are by acknowledged geniuses, such as Nam June Paik. Another example is a small gouache done by Sol LeWitt. Some of the works are by artists such as Chemiakin, who are probably not widely known outside of the area of those interested in Russian art.

One example of a previously obscure artist represented in our collection is Malik Sidibe. A photographer from Mali, he was recently given a Golden Lion Award for Lifetime Achievement at the Venice Biennale.

We enjoy being surrounded by creative impressions of life and the world. Many of the artists in our collection are individuals who have made outstanding contributions to art and to art history. We are sensitive to the reality that the works own us more than we own the works, and we are particularly sensitive to our role as mere custodians of the works, for however long this can occur.

We welcome this opportunity to share our works with others.

Paul Mansheim

Contemporary, Cool and Collected has been a highly collaborative exhibition since its inception. For their support of this exhibition and publication, I am grateful to Phil Kline, Executive Director, and Charles Mo, Chief Curator of Fine Arts, who both recognize the project's far-reaching implications for education and cultural enrichment. Heartfelt thanks are extended to all lenders to the exhibition, listed on page iv. Their enthusiastic support and willingness to share important works, some of which are fragile and unwieldy, have been key to the success of this endeavor.

A number of colleagues both at The Mint Museums and at many other institutions have been instrumental in putting me in contact with collectors and artists and have thereby assisted in framing the concepts and contents of the show. Working with such inspiring partners has also been one of the pleasures of assembling this show. I would like to extend my sincerest gratitude to the following individuals: Mary Edith Alexander, Kate Baillon-Case, Allen Blevins, Carol Cole Levin, Jim Craig, Linda Johnson Dougherty, Suzanne Hall, Brooks Johnson, Ashley Kistler, Lillian Lambrechts, Joie Lassiter, Mark Leach, Lynn Marsden-Atlass, Jerald Melberg, Dennis Oleksuk, Allison Perkins, John Ravenal, Allison Slaby, Leah Stoddard, Jonathan Stuhlman, and Brad Thomas.

Art history majors Laura Bickford and Emily

Boone volunteered at the museum while on their summer break from school. Laura and Emily, along with Library Assistant Shawn Reynolds, agreed to write entries for this catalogue. The many hours they devoted to this project were productive and their eagerness, tenacity and insights were refreshing.

Robert Hobbs contributed scholarly insights into the process of collecting the art of our time, and I thank him for his thoughtful essay. A number of the lenders to the exhibition also wrote about the joys and challenges of collecting contemporary art, which has enriched this publication. Additional thanks go to Graphic Design Manager Emily Walker, who imaginatively and skillfully created this publication. I also thank Development Officer Rosemary Martin for her meticulous copy editing. Kimberly Thomas, Curatorial Assistant, coordinated all photography and rights and reproductions for this catalogue, a task she handled with grace and good humor. I relied heavily on the staffs of institutions and commercial galleries for providing photographic materials, and these individuals are acknowledged in the Photo Credits (p. 149). Librarian Joyce Weaver shared many helpful insights and, along with Associate Registrar Kristen Watts, aided me in locating numerous research materials for this publication.

Associate Registar Katherine Steiner Stocker, the registrar for this project, lent her wit, skill and ingenuity in managing the cumbersome task of getting all of the works to the museum safely and on time. Registrar Martha Mayberry and Registration Assistants Eric Speer and Andrea Collins also contributed their talents to this exhibition. Head of Design and Installation Kurt Warnke, along with his talented associates, Leah Blackburn, William Lipscomb and Mitch Francis, created an elegant and lively installation.

Special thanks go to The Mint Museums staff members who were supportive and attentive in all aspects of the project: Courtenay Jackson, Director of Development; Betsy Gantt, Corporate Development Manager (who secured the generous sponsorship of Goodrich Foundation); Regan Jones, Director of Major Gifts; Joanna Rice, Database Coordinator; Emily Spratt, Membership Coordinator; Cheryl A. Palmer, Director of Education; Carolyn Mints, Community Relations Director; Leslie Strauss, Family Programs Coordinator; Allison Taylor, Adult Programs Coordinator; Rita Shumaker, Master Teacher; Joel Smeltzer, School Programs Coordinator; Chris Lalley, Tour Coordinator; Fred Dabney, Marketing Advisor; Pat Viser, Membership Manager; C. Michael Smith, Chief Financial Officer; M. Hannah Pickering, Accountant; Lois L. Schneider, Accountant; Natasha Rider, former Public Relations Manager and Joelle Karout, Interim Public Relations Manager; John

West, Information Technology Manager; Sandy Fisher, Manager of Retail Operations; Carol Spencer, Front Desk Coordinator; David Klingel, Special Events Manager; and Hank McKiernan, Facilities Administrator.

Contemporary, Cool and Collected was sponsored by the Goodrich Foundation. Members of the Contemporary Coalition also contributed to the publication of this catalogue. I am grateful for the additional support generously provided by Thomas E. Kanes and Susan Valentine Kanes, Emily and Zach Smith and Walter S. Brown, Jr.

For their patience, love and support, I thank D. David Childress and Helena Hanzal Childress.

Carla M. Hanzal

Patricia Anderson: Image Courtesy of the Artist

Charles Arnoldi: Image Courtesy of the Artist

Richard Avedon: © 2007 The Richard Avedon Foundation

Stephan Balkenhol:
Trohn, photograph by David Ramsey
Untitled (woman), photograph by David Ramsey
Untitled (man), Image Courtesy of Galeria Pepe Cobo,
Madrid, Spain
© 2007 Artists Rights Society (ARS), New York /
VG Bild-Kunst, Bonn

Romare Bearden: Image Courtesy of Jerald Melberg Gallery
Art © Romare Bearden Foundation / Licensed by VAGA,
New York, New York

Carole Benzaken: photograph by David Ramsey
© 2007 Artists Rights Society (ARS), New York / ADAGP, Paris

Janet Biggs: Image Courtesy of the Artist

Jeff Brouws:
Mobil / Trailer, Inyokern, California, and
Playland, Rye, New York
©Jeff Brouws/Courtesy Robert Mann Gallery, New York.

Edward Burtynsky:
*Rock of Ages #8, Abandoned Section, Wells-Lamson Quarry,
Barre, VT* and *Shipbreaking #27, Chittagong, Bangladesh*
Images Courtesy of the Artist and Robert Koch Gallery,
San Francisco

Sir Anthony Caro: photograph by Tom Landen

Chuck Close: Image Courtesy of Pace Prints

Gregory Crewdson: Image Courtesy of the Artist and Luhring
Augustine, New York

Willem de Kooning: Image Courtesy of Leslie Sacks Fine Art
© 2007 The Willem de Kooning Foundation / Artists Rights
Society (ARS), New York

Richard Diebenkorn: Image Courtesy of Sotheby's, New York

Tara Donovan: Image Courtesy of Ace Gallery

Lalla Essaydi: photograph by David Ramsey
Image Courtesy of the Artist and Schneider Gallery,
Chicago, Illinois

Helen Frankenthaler:
Denominator and *The Fourth*, photographs by Tom Landen

Sam Francis: photograph by David Ramsey

Eric Freeman: Image Courtesy of Mary Boone Gallery, New York

Wyatt Gallery: Image Courtesy of the Artist

Rimma Gerlovina and Valeriy Gerlovin: Image Courtesy of Lisa
Sette Gallery, Scottsdale, Arizona

Robert Gober: *Untitled (shoe)* and *Newspaper* (*Hare Escobar.,/
Wedding*)
photographs by Adam Reich, Courtesy of the Artist and
Matthew Marks Gallery, New York

Anthony Goicolea: *Pool Pushers* and *Smoke Stack*
Images Courtesy of Postmasters Gallery, New York, New York

Andy Goldsworthy: photograph by David Ramsey

Hoss Haley: Image courtesy of the Artist and Joie Lassiter Gallery

David Hilliard: Image Courtesy of Yancey Richardson Gallery

Hans Hofmann: photograph by David Ramsey
© 2007 The Hans Hofmann Trust / Artists Rights Society (ARS), New York

Herb Jackson: photograph by David Ramsey

Josef Koudelka: Image Courtesy of the Artist and Magnum Photos

Jonathan Lasker: Image Courtesy of the Artist and Cheim & Read, New York

Charles LeDray: Image Courtesy of Sperone Westwater, New York

Hung Liu: Image Courtesy of Rena Bransten Gallery, San Francisco, CA

Loretta Lux: *Girl with Crossed Arms* and *Isabella*
© Loretta Lux, Courtesy Yossi Milo Gallery
© 2007 Artists Rights Society (ARS), New York / VG Bild-Kunst, Bonn

Sally Mann: *Untitled (Deep South #5)* and *Virginia at Nine*
© Sally Mann. Images Courtesy of Jackson Fine Art Gallery, Atlanta, GA
Untitled, from the Mother Land: Virginia Series
© Sally Mann. Courtesy Gagosian Gallery, New York
Jessie Bites © Sally Mann. Courtesy Gagosian Gallery, New York

Tom McGrath: Image Courtesy of the Artist and Zach Feuer Gallery, New York

Jason Meadows: Image Courtesy of Marc Foxx, Los Angeles

Joan Mitchell: photograph by David Ramsey

Phil Moody: Image Courtesy of Joie Lassiter Gallery, Charlotte, NC

Andrew Moore: Image Courtesy of Yancey Richardson Gallery, New York

Robert Motherwell: Image Courtesy of Jerald Melberg Gallery
Art © Dedalus Foundation, Inc. / Licensed by VAGA, New York, New York

Vik Muniz: Image Courtesy of Rena Bransten Gallery, San Francisco
Art © Vik Muniz / Licensed by VAGA, New York, New York

Elizabeth Murray: Image Courtesy of Bank of America Collection

Kenneth Noland: photograph by Tom Landon
Art © Kenneth Noland / Licensed by VAGA, New York, New York

Deborah Oropallo:
Image Courtesy of Stephen Wirtz Gallery, San Francisco, CA

Tony Oursler: Image Courtesy of the Artist and Lehmann Maupin Gallery, New York

Nam June Paik: photograph by Chris Gomien
Image Courtesy of Carl Solway Gallery, Cincinnati, Ohio

Robert and Shana ParkeHarrison: Image Courtesy of the Artist

Judy Pfaff: Courtesy of Tandem Press and Joie Lassiter Gallery, Charlotte, NC
Art © Judy Pfaff / Licensed by VAGA, New York, New York

Sarah Pickering: Image Courtesy of Daniel Cooney Fine Art, New York

Liliana Porter: Images Courtesy of the Artist

Michael Prince: Image Courtesy of the Artist

Stephanie Pryor: Image Courtesy of ACME Gallery, Los Angeles, California

Susan Rothenberg: Image Courtesy of Sperone Westwater, New York
© 2007 Susan Rothenberg / Artist Rights Society (ARS), New York

Michal Rovner: Photograph by Kerry Ryan McFate,
Courtesy PaceWilderstein, New York
© 2007 Michal Rovner / Artists Rights Society (ARS), New York

Alison Saar: Image Courtesy of the Artist

Tom Sachs: Image Courtesy of the Artist and Galerie
    Thaddaeus Ropac

Lorna Simpson: Image Courtesy of Albright-Knox Gallery

Donald Sultan: photograph by David Ramsey

Mark Tobey: photograph by David Ramsey

Kara Walker: photograph by David Ramsey

We sincerely thank the following individuals for assisting with securing photography for this publication:

Mary Edith Alexander- Bank of America, Charlotte, NC

Dean Anes- ACME, Los Angeles, CA

Jenny Baie- Rena Bransten Gallery, San Francisco, CA

Guillaume Benaich- Galerie Thassaeus Ropac, Paris, France

Courtney Booth and Nina del Rio- Sotheby's, New York

Jennifer Burbank- Sperone Westwater, New York

Caroline Burghardt- Luhring Augustine, New York

Brian Camp- Robert Koch Gallery, San Francisco, CA

Claudia Carson- Robert Gober Studio, New York

Julie Casemore- Stephaen Wirtz Gallery, San Francisco, CA

Dana Claudat- Ace Gallery, Los Angeles

Celine Cleron- Galerie Nathalie Obadia, Paris, France

Daniel Cooney- Daniel Cooney Fine Art, New York

Anita Douthat- Solway Gallery, Cincinnati, OH

Grace Evans- Zach Feuer Gallery (LFL), New York

Rachel Flax- Robert Mann Gallery, New York

Carolyn Francis and James McKee- Gagosian Gallery, New York

Michelle Franco- The Richard Avedon Foundation, New York

Isabel Garcia de Castro- Galeria Pepe Cobo, Madrid, Spain

Rodney Hill- Marc Foxx, Los Angeles, CA

Bettina Hilleckes- Gallery Springer-Winckler, Berlin, Germany

Tom Hughes- Albright-Knox Art Gallery, Buffalo, NY

Gaybe Johnson, Chris Clamp and Jerald Melberg- Jerald
Melberg Gallery, Charlotte, NC

Stephanie Joson and Lindsay Macdonald- Galerie Lelong,
    New York

Yossi Milo and Christina Freeman- Yossi Milo Gallery

Temma Nanas- Leslie Sacks Fine Art, Los Angeles

Christina O'Keefe Aptowicz- Artists Rights Society (ARS),
    New York

Heather Palmer- Pace Wilderstein, New York

Irene Roughton- Chrysler Museum of Art, Norfolk, VA

Magdalena Sawon- Postmasters Gallery, New York

Amber Shields- Cheim & Read, New York

Marcus Shubert- Office of Edward Burtynsky, Toronto,
    Ontario, Canada

Michael Shulman- Magnum Photos Inc., New York

Irina Toshkova and Joie Lassiter- Joie Lassiter Gallery,
    Charlotte, NC

Christina Turley- Matthew Marks Gallery, New York